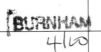

CW00516750

Get Over Your
Break-up

Hodder Arnold

MEMBER OF THE HODDER HEADLINE GROUP

Get Over Your
Break-up

Nicci Talbot
Edited by Denise Robertson

A MEMBER OF THE HODDER HEADLINE GROUP

Essex County Council Libraries

Orders: Please contact Bookpoint Ltd, 130 Milton Park, Abingdon, Oxon OX14 4SB. Telephone: +44 (0) 1235 827720. Fax: +44 (0) 1235 400454. Lines are open 09.00 to 5.00, Monday to Saturday, with a 24-hour message answering service. You can also order through our website www.hoddereducation.co.uk.

British Library Cataloguing in Publication Data
A catalogue record for this title is available from the British Library.

ISBN-13: 978 0 340 94319 9

First published   2007
Impression number 10 9 8 7 6 5 4 3 2 1
Year   2012 2011 2010 2009 2008 2007

Typeset by Transet Limited, Coventry, England.
Printed in Great Britain for Hodder Education, a division of Hodder Headline, an Hachette Livre UK Company, 338 Euston Road, London, NW1 3BH, by Cox & Wyman Ltd, Reading, Berkshire.

Hodder Headline's policy is to use papers that are natural, renewable and recyclable products and made from wood grown in sustainable forests. The logging and manufacturing processes are expected to conform to the environmental regulations of the country of origin.

ABOUT THE AUTHORS

Nicci Talbot is a freelance writer specializing in sex and relationships and health and wellbeing. She is the author of *Orgasm* and *Unzipped*, and *Movie Star Magic* – a beauty book for girls. She lives in Guernsey with her family.

Denise Robertson's television career began with *BBC Breakfast Time* in 1984. She has been the resident agony aunt of ITV's *This Morning* for the last 20 years. In that time she has received over 200,000 letters covering a wide range of problems from viewers and from readers of her newspaper and magazine columns. She has written 19 novels and several works of non-fiction. Her autobiography, *Agony: Don't Get Me Started,* was published in paperback by Little Books in July 2007. She is associated with many charities, among them Relate, The Bubble Foundation, Careline and the National Council for the Divorced and Separated.

ACKNOWLEDGEMENTS

The author would like to thank the following contacts and organizations for useful research material:

Books:
After The Affair (Relate Relationships), by Julia Cole, (Random House, 2001)
Starting Again: How To Learn From The Past For A Better Future, (Relate Relationships) by Sarah Litvinoff, (Random House, 2001).

Websites:
www.armchairadvice.org.uk – relationship breakdown advice
www.bbc.co.uk/health – lifestyle, relationships and health information
www.careforthefamily.org.uk – charity helping those hurting because of family breakdown
www.channel4.com/health – information about couples' counselling, family breakdown, relationships and health for adults and teens
www.cri.org.uk – Crime Reduction Initiatives: Open The Door On Domestic Abuse. Support, treatment and rehabilitation services.

www.insidedivorce.com – legal advice for divorcees

www.sheknows.com – relationship advice & break up survival guide

www.shelter.org.uk – housing and your rights

www.sfla.co.uk – legal advice site. Telling your friends and family about divorce.

www.therelationshipgym.com – relationships and dating advice

www.wespsych.com – couples' counselling and relationship advice from psychologist Nancy Wesson

WHICH PAGE?

I'm not sure whether to stay or go. Would a trial separation help? *Turn to page 64.*

How can I tell my family and children? *Turn to page 123.*

I don't have money to spend on a solicitor – would mediation help? *Turn to page 94.*

I'm worried I won't be able to cope financially if we split up. *Turn to page 82.*

I feel so lonely on my own. *Turn to page 138.*

How do I go about getting child maintenance? *Turn to page 100.*

I was with my husband for years, how do I begin to start dating again? *Turn to page 201.*

How will we manage the children? Who will have custody? *Turn to page 107*

Thanks to everybody who shared their stories
with me for this book. To Linda Jones at
Brethertons LLP, Sally McLaughlin at Relate,
Dr David Hewison at the Tavistock Centre for
Couple Relationships, Sandy Hutchinson Nunns
at the Institute of Transactional Analysis,
Victoria Roddam at Hodder Education, and to
Matthew Noble for all his support.

Nicci Talbot, 2007

CONTENTS

FOREWORD

By Fern Britton and Phillip Schofield

As presenters of ITV's *This Morning*, over many years we have met many incredible people with many incredible stories to tell. What we have learnt is that life can be wonderful but it can also be very hard.

Our phone-ins have generated thousands of calls a day from viewers all over Great Britain looking for suitable advice on a range of subjects. What is very obvious from these calls is that we are not alone with the personal challenges we often face and there is a great need for help in dealing with them. We are always cheered by the follow-up letters and emails from viewers saying how our experts' advice has helped them to turn their lives around.

Over the 20 years *This Morning* has been on air, Denise Robertson, our agony aunt, has regularly offered support and advice to millions of viewers on a huge range of personal problems and she spends even more time off-screen answering letters, calling those in distress and dealing with questions via the internet. As a result, she is uniquely qualified to edit these books which reflect the common sense and sensitive advice that we provide on the show.

We believe these survival guides will help you to deal with the practical and emotional fall-out caused by issues such as bereavement, relationship break-ups, debt, infertility, addiction, domestic violence and depression.

If you feel that your particular problems are insurmountable – don't! There is always a way to improve your life or at least get yourself on a path towards a new start. If you think you are alone with your problem – don't! Our experience shows that many of us face the same problems but are often reluctant to admit it. You have already made a great start by picking up this book.

We both wish you all the strength and support you need to tackle your own personal problems and sincerely hope we can help through these books and through our continued work on the programme.

INTRODUCTION

There's nothing nicer than opening a letter which begins 'A year ago you told me I'd be happy again. I didn't believe you. Now I know you were right'.

The end of a relationship can feel like the end of the world because for months, even years, you've had someone to share your life with. In reality it's only the end of a chapter. However painful it may be – and I'd be the first to acknowledge it can hurt like hell – there's always another page to turn and a new chapter to begin.

Sometimes a fear of the unknown can keep you in a relationship which has lost all its sparkle, even the last remnants of love. The thought of being alone can be scary, even when you have supportive friends and family. The phrase 'Nature abhors a vacuum' is soundly based but the end of something which, however lovely it was, now only brings you pain will give you room to rebuild.

This book is designed to help you decide whether or not it's time to go, how to manage the break-up if it's inevitable and, most importantly, how to begin again. Follow its advice and one day you may be writing one of those letters that begins 'You told me I would be happy again ... you were right'.

Denise Robertson

HOW THIS BOOK WILL HELP YOU

Breaking up with a partner can be devastating. It doesn't matter whether you've been together for ten days or ten years – it still hurts. Relationships are an emotional investment. You invest your time, energy and love and you expect those things in return. You go into them hoping for the best, that you've met 'the one' and will live happily ever after. Then life happens and your relationship is put to the test. The strongest ones survive and others fall away, to make room for something else.

If you've picked up this book in despair because you're going through a break-up right now, your life, as you know it, has changed forever. Your long-term plans are no longer relevant and you're trying to come to terms with your new single status. No matter how independent you are this is a shock when you've been part of a team for so long. Your partner was your 'rock' – someone you could moan to about your day and ask for a cuddle. Often, it's the little things that hit us when they're gone. Like finding an old T-shirt that still smells of them, or finding yourself cooking their favourite dish. It's especially hard if you didn't see the break-up coming, if you were coasting along quite happily and your partner announced it out of the blue.

No doubt your emotions are all over the place right now. You're worrying about all sorts – how you're going to cope with work, family, children – as well as churning things over in your mind about what went wrong. We all deal with grief in different ways. You might feel like lying in bed and eating junk food or you might feel like doing something physical to vent your anger. Both reactions are normal. Break-ups happen every day, to millions of people, and remember that however lonely you feel right now, you're not alone.

When you're in the thick of it though, it can seem like the end of the world. And in some ways, it is. It's the end of the old you and the start of something new. Break-ups are also about new beginnings – a time for you to change and grow as a person and to rediscover who you are, to develop your interests and meet new people. No relationship, however short-lived, is ever a waste of time because we learn from all of them. It's human nature to dwell on the bad bits and dismiss it as 'a lie', 'a sham' or 'a waste of time' if things ended badly. If you find yourself feeling this way try not to blame the other person. Taking responsibility for your part in it is empowering and it will help you to move on and form better, stronger and more fulfilling relationships in the future.

This book is for men and women who are going through a break-up, be it of a marriage or a long-term relationship. Your circumstances may be different but you do have one thing in common – you're looking for ways to deal with your feelings and move on. The first part of the book will explore how you're feeling right now, the lifecycle of a relationship and some common reasons why they break down. We've put together a survival plan for the first month, to get you through the worst of it, and there's a chapter covering the practical things you need to sort out immediately like money and a place to live.

Part 2 expands on this, looking at the first few months after a break-up, how you'll be feeling now. Here the emphasis is on *you*, and on creating a new identity and rebuilding your self-esteem as it will have taken a bit of a hammering.

Part 3 covers longer-term emotional and practical issues – getting through the first year, which people often say is the toughest. Birthdays, anniversaries, holidays and other little reminders can be hard to deal with. You'll also be thinking about your future goals and whether or not you want to form a new relationship.

Part 4 has lots of inspiring stories and messages of hope from people just like you, who have been through a break-up and come out the other side.

Part 5 provides a comprehensive list of useful resources – organizations, books and websites to help you deal with the practicalities.

Whatever stage you're at right now, you can dip into this book whenever you feel you need a bit of support. We know what it's like and we're here for you.

The important thing to remember is that you are constantly changing. You aren't the same person now as you were this morning and you won't be the same person tomorrow. **You are stronger than you think.** Grieving isn't a linear process and some days will be good and others bad so don't expect too much of yourself. Be kind to yourself. By the time you finish this book you will be a whole new person looking at things with renewed excitement and possibility.

Part 1: What to Do Right Now

1

Where you are now, where you will be soon

In this chapter we're going to look at how you're feeling right now, this minute. We'll look at common fears and worries and things you can do to start moving forwards. The first step in recovery is regaining a sense of control and you've made a start by reading this book. It will help you to make sense of your situation and how you're feeling. We've also put together some ideas for things you can do today to make yourself feel better. So, come on, let's work out where you are now and think about making some positive changes.

How do I feel today?

Here is a list of emotions that you might be feeling right now. They are all normal and healthy. What's important is to acknowledge what has happened and how you are feeling. Feelings are transient and in a few days' time they will have changed, so don't try to fight them. Going through the 'heartbreak' is an essential part of the grieving process. No one reacts to grief in the same way.

Tick any emotions that apply to you right now and then redo this exercise in a week's time.

❑ Confused

❑ Angry

❑ Jealous

❑ Bitter

❑ Tearful

❑ Scared

❑ Numb

❑ On autopilot

❑ Withdrawn

❑ Relieved

❏ Shattered

❏ Indifferent

❏ Panicked

❏ Worried

❏ Embarrassed

❏ Resentful

❏ Ashamed

❏ A failure

❏ In denial

❏ Disbelieving

How did you do? Don't worry if there are lots of ticks. Your immediate feelings will be the most painful and these will pass. Doing this exercise might seem a bit silly but it helps you to process and think about how you are feeling.

Survival tips

Try to remember that:

- You're not alone

- You won't feel this way forever

- It's okay to do nothing right now

- You can let yourself grieve for what has gone

- You don't have to make any important decisions today

- You will be happy again soon.

Take things one day at a time and don't expect too much of yourself right now. Here are some things you can do today to help yourself feel better:

- Go for a walk in the countryside – exercise will make you feel a lot better.

- Call a close friend or your mum or dad and explain what has happened.

- Spend time on your own if you want to.

- Start writing a diary to explore your feelings. It helps to get your thoughts on paper. Doing it first thing can give a positive start to the day.

- Spend five minutes a day relaxing and meditating – close your eyes and breathe in and out until you can feel your body relaxing.

- Read a poem about love and loss.

- Cook yourself something you've never had before and eat it slowly, really tasting each mouthful. Try to eat small meals every couple of hours to keep your strength up even if you don't feel like it.

- Go for a massage – touch is very important for your health and wellbeing.

Q. When will I feel normal again?

A. You will probably feel low for the first couple of weeks. After that, the fog will lift and you'll start feeling more like your old self. You'll start to rationalize things a bit and work out what you want to do next. This is a turning point as it means you're thinking independently of your own future rather than of you as a couple. The pain won't go away immediately but it will become easier to bear and there are lots of things you can do to speed that process up. Try to take it one day at a time and concentrate on spending some quality time with yourself and doing things that you enjoy.

Breathing exercise

Here is a breathing technique that will help you to de-stress. Try and practise it twice a day or whenever you feel yourself getting stressed.

1 Lie on the bed with your arms by your side and close your eyes. Have the window open or put on some relaxing music.

2 Take a deep breath in and tense the muscles in your feet, holding for five seconds. Breathe out and relax.

3 Repeat this action, working your way up from your feet to the top of your head.

4 Once you reach the top put your hands on your tummy and take a few deep breaths. It might feel a little odd at first because we normally breathe quite shallowly from our lungs. Your body isn't used to taking in so much oxygen.

5 Whenever you feel yourself getting upset and stressed put your hands on your tummy and repeat the deep breathing exercise – it's a signal to your body that you need to calm down.

Q. It's been six months since we split and I'm still dwelling on things. What can I do?

A. Did you and your ex talk things over properly to resolve what happened? Sometimes it can be harder to overcome grief when things are left unsaid and you don't really know what went wrong. You keep going over the same ground, thinking about what you did or didn't do and don't come to any conclusions. Make a list of what is bothering you, what you still need to know and talk to your ex if you can. If that's not possible write him or her a letter explaining your feelings – you don't have to post it. Keep yourself busy and make sure you have plenty to look forward to in your diary. If you're really struggling it may help to talk to a counsellor to get a different perspective.

I found it very hard to talk about how I was feeling after my wife left me. It came out of the blue and I didn't deal with it very well at all. I felt very angry most days and the split was messy. Looking back on it I realize I bottled up my anger and there was no one I could really talk to about how I was feeling. There's an idea that men aren't supposed to talk about their feelings or cry or show any emotion, which I think does you more harm in the long run. It stops you getting on with your life. Eventually I heard about a workshop where I could meet other people going through a break-up and it saw me through. I felt so much better after talking about what was going on.

Jack

*I refused to see the warning signs that
we weren't compatible. He was quite a
cold, emotionally detached person and
I'm a 'touchy feely' person who needs
warmth and reassurance in a
relationship. At the age of 34 I can
finally admit that without feeling
neurotically needy! I was 29 when we
split up and he was 27 and I was
panicking that I was fast approaching
30. I had visions of me as Miss
Haversham! I can see now that I was
just grasping at straws to hang on to
him because I thought I wanted to settle
down and have kids and that it might be
too late to start over with someone else.*

*The problem with burying your head
in the sand is that your self-esteem takes
a nosedive and at times I questioned my
sanity rather than faced up to the fact
that my relationship just wasn't
bringing out the best in me. Looking
back, my advice would be not to take so
long noticing someone's faults and to get
out of a destructive situation while you
can. I think of it as a slice of cake – the
problem starts off at the tip as small but*

as time goes by the problems get bigger and bigger.

I also think it's a bad idea to sleep with someone too soon. Get to know them first, as a friend and ask yourself if you actually like them. Do they bring out the best in you? Do you have a laugh together? Do they look out for you or are they just after one thing? Work out what your incompatibilities are before you get emotionally involved. Some men don't fully value women they haven't had to work hard to get! You need to bubble wrap your heart and stay rational about the relationship until you decide if you are both compatible.

After two years of getting nowhere I gave him the red card because my biological clock was ticking and after asking him if he saw a future with me he said he wasn't sure. He has since met someone else and is getting married this autumn and I'm still single but I'm glad that I didn't rush into anything. Looking back it made me miserable and it would have been a loveless, resentful and cold marriage.

Getting over someone isn't just a 'matter of time' – it's about quality time doing stuff that you've always wanted or meant to do. About having goals of your own that give you a sense of achievement whether it's running a marathon or finally buying a place of your own. It's also about kissing a few frogs and princes and not being afraid to be choosy. The best tonic is getting back in touch with all of your old mates and having a good cry, rant or bitch and realizing that you're not the only one. Then get back out there and meet someone that you truly deserve.

Ella

In the next chapter we're going to look in more detail at why relationships fail and how the changes in society have contributed towards this.

2

Why do relationships fail?

We are all under greater pressure nowadays at work and home and this is reflected in the growing number of divorces and break-ups. The number of people getting married has fallen and more of us cohabit with our partners, with or without children, or live alone. We are building careers before having children – if at all. It's a huge struggle to get on the property ladder and so we make compromises, working longer hours or living with friends and family to make ends meet.

Many women work full-time in addition to raising a family and some of you earn more than your partners, which can cause tension in a partnership, as men are traditionally the 'hunter gatherers'. Women get fed up with being expected to be super mums and look after a partner as well. They are not so worried about surviving financially on their own because they may have a little nest egg squirrelled away.

On the television it can seem as if everyone is having great sex and it's enough to make you feel inadequate. Some of you have affairs because you're not sexual with your partners anymore or you're curious to know what it would be like with someone else. Magazine articles are full of tips on 'how to be sexy' and 'how to raise your libido' and it can make us feel like there's something wrong because we don't feel sexy all the time. In the soaps people split up and get together with someone else straight away. It can leave us with unrealistic expectations as to how quickly we are supposed to get over someone and we may find ourselves getting into new relationships on the rebound.

We're going to look at some of the possible causes for your crisis in a bit more detail, starting with a big issue – infidelity.

Affairs

Affairs can have a huge impact on your relationship. For one thing, the trust has gone. You probably held your partner on a pedestal, in high esteem and then you find out they have been unfaithful. It is devastating and it can feel like your whole relationship has been one fat lie. Most people think affairs are wrong and it's difficult to say how many people have them because there isn't any proper research on this. Affairs mean different things to different people. Here's a checklist – what do you think counts as infidelity?

❏ Kissing someone else

❏ Having an anonymous fantasy affair by text or email

❏ Having sex with someone else when you're drunk

❏ Spending time with your ex

❏ Looking at other men and women in the street

❏ Thinking about having sex with someone else.

How did you do? If you asked a friend to do this exercise he or she would probably have a completely different response from you. We all have different boundaries and what is acceptable to one person might be totally out of bounds for another. Affairs happen for a reason and however painful it may be you need to examine the state of your relationship at the time. Try to work out if any of your actions were accountable. It's tempting to ignore our own behaviour and blame our partner but if you don't get to the root of the problem you will go on to attract similar people and relationships in the future.

Survival tip

Taking responsibility for your own actions is empowering and it means that you won't remain a victim.

---

*Here are some common reasons why affairs
happen. Tick any that apply to you.*

❏ You have a stressful life at home and the affair
is an escape from that. It makes you feel
young, sexy and alive.

❏ You travel a lot for work and use the internet
at the end of the day to unwind. You've met
several people for fantasy sex online and have
occasionally texted people. It's a fun
distraction and it allows you to indulge your
fantasies a bit. You don't see the harm in it
because you'd never meet them in real life and
you're in a good relationship anyway.

❏ You're a bit scared of settling down with your
partner. What if she's not 'the one'? She wants
to get married but you're holding back and
making excuses. You prefer to keep your
options open.

❏ You still see your ex from time to time but you
wouldn't tell your partner as he'd hit the roof.

❏ Your relationship has been sexually dead for a
long time but you're good companions and for
the sake of the children you're staying
together. You have an 'agreement' in that you

can both take a lover as long as it's discreet and no one else will find out. Somehow this seems to take the pressure off a bit and you're getting on a lot better.

You probably identified with a few of the emotions in the checklist in Chapter 1 (pages 6–7). Finding out that a partner has been unfaithful is devastating but, in a positive light, it is a symptom of the fact that you both need to make changes within the relationship if it is to continue. It can be very hard to admit to yourself that it might have been caused by something you did or didn't do. Have a think about how things are in the relationship – sexually and emotionally. How much time are you spending together? What are your working patterns like? Do you communicate well? Have either of you allowed another area of your life to dominate things?

Should I stay or go?

This depends on your circumstances and feelings about infidelity and how you found out about the affair. Consider these points before you make a decision.

- Was it just sexual?

- Was it a 'one-off' or has it been going on for years?

- Have either of you been unfaithful before? Did you get through it? What did you learn?

- Has your partner shown remorse and a desire to end the affair?

- How do you both feel about infidelity? Do you think it can be overcome?

- How trustworthy is your partner in other areas of the relationship? Does he/she let you down anywhere else?

- What was the state of your relationship at the time? How accountable were you for what happened?

This is a lot to take on board so don't rush things but take as much time as you need – there is no point trying to think clearly and rationally if you're still het up and upset. Meet up with your partner to talk about things when you feel ready. Set a time limit and let him/her explain and tell their story without interrupting. Consider seeking independent advice from a counsellor or therapist.

Deciding to stay

If you've talked it over and believe the relationship is worth saving then you can build on things to become a stronger team. Keep writing your diary pages to help you to process what has happened and to help you let go of any anger or resentment. Don't expect to forgive and forget straight away. You might not feel you can do that for a while. Take small steps each day to rebuild the trust which has been shattered.

Have a think about ways to improve the relationship. For example:

- Can you both cut back on your responsibilities to spend more time together?

- Can you take up a new hobby together – something fun and active that gets you outdoors so you've got more to talk about than domestics?

- Check in with each other throughout the day – a short phone call, text message or email to say 'I'm thinking of you' can make you both feel loved and needed.

- Arrange to go away for a few nights to spend quality time together. Making time for each other is the difference between a couple who exist and a couple who are growing together.

- Think of each other as strangers – this can re-inject some of the initial excitement you both felt when you met.

- Try not to assume you know everything about your partner but ask him/her what he/she would like to do. You might be surprised!

If sex was the reason for the affair then consider going for counselling and sex therapy. This can help you to work out what your attitudes towards sex are. You might be given some non-sensate exercises to do – lots of physical contact but no sex, to help you reconnect as a couple. Contact Relate or the British Association for Sexual and Relationship Therapy (BASRT) – details of which are given in Part 5.

Remember that you can't erase the past. All you can do is learn from it and try to focus on your partner's behaviour from this point, rather than dwell on the past.

Deciding to go

If you're too angry and hurt to stay in the house or feel that the relationship cannot be salvaged then call a friend or family member to be with you. You'll need to sort the practicalities first – a place to stay and some money while you work out what to do next. Don't make any hasty decisions while you're upset. Instead arrange a time to talk to your partner once you feel ready.

Growing apart

You met at school. You were deliriously in love, desperate to move in together and have babies. And there's nothing wrong with that at all. Some of the happiest relationships start out that way and are still going strong! But for some of you, things change. Your needs have changed and you're not sure if your relationship now fulfils them. Perhaps you have other goals such as travel or studying for a new career. You feel held back by your relationship and you're starting to feel niggled by the little things your partner does. You can feel yourself pulling away from the relationship and trying to create a little distance.

Your twenties are a time of discovery and about finding out who you are and what you want from life. Things change in a short space of time – there's college or university, new jobs, promotion, moving house. You're meeting new people and, potentially, new partners and it's very easy to drift as a couple if you aren't keeping in touch with each other's needs. Sometimes nothing is really wrong. The relationship is fine but you're both slightly bored and wondering what else might be out there. Couples who marry young are much more likely to split up than those who get together later in life.

You might be feeling:

- A little sad – he/she was your first love and you had some happy times together.

- Indifferent.

- A bit overwhelmed. You've been joined at the hip for so long, it's hard to imagine doing things by yourself again.

- Relieved – you both know it's been a long time coming.

MYTH: Men get over affairs much more quickly than women.

FACT: How long it takes to get over a break-up depends on your emotional make-up and not on your gender.

Deciding whether to stay or go

You both know if there's any future in the relationship. If you're not sure if this is just a phase then think about taking a break from each other for a while to do your own thing – go travelling, study, see other people and see how you both feel in a year's time. Time will give you perspective on things. If boredom is an issue then make an effort and plan three fun things to do together this week.

If you've decided to move on but want to remain good friends then make an effort to stay in touch with each other and your families. We all need friends who know us well and can advise us on future things.

Now we are going to look at some of the major life changes that can affect our personal relationships.

Starting a family

A baby will often enhance a relationship and make it stronger, although in the early stages it can have a big impact as you both adjust to your new roles and responsibilities. Things may become a little bit harder to deal with when you're tired from endless feeds and nappy changes. In some cases people feel less satisfied with their personal relationships after a baby is born. This evens out when a child goes to school but can dip again once they reach their teenage years.

A baby can sometimes mean:

- You have less time for each other as a couple

- One of you, usually Dad, may feel left out and jealous of all the attention lavished on the baby

- A lack of sleep and sex

- Conflict over parenting styles between families

- Coming to terms with your new roles and perhaps missing your old life

- Loss of freedom – the same routines can be stifling

- Conflict over who brings the money in and who is at home. A woman might miss the social contact of work if she's at home on her own all day.

What you can do

Give yourselves time to adapt to the new situation and don't try and take on too much in the first few months. Set a date to have a cosy evening together without your baby. Make sure that you both keep talking about how you're feeling and don't let things build up. Make time for each other during the day – a cup of tea, a gesture, a word of thanks will be appreciated. Try not to criticize each other's parenting styles – we all do things differently and there is no right or wrong way to bring up your baby. If you've been feeling a bit low, see your doctor or health visitor to have a chat about things. It doesn't matter how slight – **it's always worth talking to someone** about how you're feeling.

A few more ideas

- It can be tempting to say 'It's your turn now.' Sometimes we can find ourselves being quite competitive after our baby is born, or feeling a bit resentful if we're doing all the work, or certain jobs fall to us. Talk to each other about it – your partner might not be hugely confident about his or her parenting skills and may avoid doing certain things for this reason. Some men are funny about handling babies – 'It's too small, I might drop it.' If that's the case then you may need to work on building his confidence.

- Plan for your baby as much as you can beforehand. Write down the impact you think he/she might have on your relationship and how you are likely to react. It will help you to feel more in control after the baby arrives.

- Consider joining a counselling group so you can meet other new mums and dads. Your doctor or health visitor will have information.

- Consider doing a course together to help prepare you for parenthood. Relate runs a workshop for partners who have become parents (see Part 5, Chapter 15).

Things may be difficult and challenging initially and over time you will find yourselves adjusting to your new role as parents. Things will settle down, and there are many happy times ahead.

Empty nesters

If you've been at home bringing up the children for years it can be a bit of shock when they leave home and you've suddenly got lots of time on your hands. Your partner still works full-time and the time you spend together seems forced because you don't really seem to have anything in common anymore. You're feeling lonely. Somewhere, along the way, 'you' got lost and life suddenly seems a bit pointless.

Relationships can break down at this point because most of us are living longer, are in better health and have more options. We can retrain for another job, travel or pursue other interests. You may also be aware of your own mortality if your parents have recently died. It can take a 'mid-life crisis' of sorts to spur us on to make changes.

Deciding whether to stay or go

It very much depends on the bond you have and whether you both want the relationship to continue. If the love is long gone and you've been together for the sake of the children then ask yourself if you want to continue living like this now they have left home. You might be scared or worried about surviving financially on your own, especially if you've been out of the job market for a few years. If this is the case there are agencies that specialize in helping people back to work after a career break.

If you share a strong bond but the passion has long gone then shake things up a bit. Think of each other as strangers again and make an effort to do new things together. Sometimes couples choose to go on holiday separately, if they have different interests. If this has been your pattern over the past few years then book something completely new to you both. There are some excellent travel agencies specializing in adventure holidays and you can learn new skills together. Do some courses to learn new skills so that you have things to talk about other than the children. This can be a very exciting time in your life. You are two again after years of being a family so it's understandable that a few adjustments will need to take place.

Redundancy

This can be a very stressful time for you both. If a man is made redundant he may feel like less of a man because he can't provide for his partner, and a woman, often subconsciously, may look to a man to be a good provider. All sorts of tensions can arise. You may resent your partner being at home under your feet. He or she might be depressed or moody and worried about getting another job. Money is tight. You're both stressed and no longer feel like being intimate.

Try to view redundancy as a positive. Hopefully it means a bit of extra money to retrain and do something else. You could think about getting a grant to start up a business together. You could take a career break and travel. There are lots of options. It can feel a bit scary because we're so used to our daily routines and we come to rely on them. If your partner seems to be depressed suggest he or she sees the doctor to get some help.

Try to avoid criticizing your partner. The best ideas come to us when we are relaxed and your partner may need a bit of down time to recoup energy and think about what to do next. Be affectionate and stay physically close so that he or she feels wanted and appreciated.

Illness

A partner's illness can put a huge strain on a relationship. All sorts of feelings arise on both sides – guilt, anger, resentment, worry, grief and confusion. If your partner has always been independent it can be very difficult when he or she is reliant on you to take care of basic needs. He or she might feel guilty about being a burden – physically and financially. You will be struggling to cope with your new role as carer and are trying to balance your needs as an individual with taking care of your partner. It can be very tough if the illness is mental and you can no longer joke or bond over past memories.

Take it one day at a time and don't expect too much of each other. Your doctor should be a great help and there are many excellent support organizations. Keep the lines of communication open and suggest a plan of action for each day so that there is some structure and a goal to achieve. You could set up a website for your partner to chart his or her progress. This is a way of staying in touch with the world and it will help your partner to feel like they are achieving something.

You may be entitled to further benefits if your partner is unable to work. See Part 5 for contacts.

Personal space

When you first fall in love you tend to do everything together as part of the bonding process. You might find yourself making compromises and doing less of the things you enjoy to make time for each other. This is fine in the short term but after a while you will both start to look for space within the relationship. You may resent your partner if he or she puts restrictions on your time and this can sometimes be a reason for a break-up. It is essential **to develop as an individual** as well as with a partner, and successful relationships find a balance so that both of your needs are being fulfilled. Couples who spend all their time together find that things become dull after a while.

Keep working on your careers and personal interests as this will reinforce your own identity within the relationship and you will have more to bring to it. When you spark off each other on a mental level it translates to the physical so you'll probably find that your sex life also improves. Sometimes you will be bored and that's fine. Boredom is transient. Make sure that you are both pursuing things that you enjoy and feel passionate about. Many mothers find that 'me time' disappears after children and this can cause resentment so make sure that you are taking time out for yourself.

Attracting the wrong type

The type of person you are attracted to is based on a combination of things. A bit of fantasy, people who had an impact on you when you were a child, your friends and your parents. Subconsciously you look for a partner who has a combination of these characteristics and this can be destructive. If your relationships are always stressful and volatile you might find that you are addicted to the drama and can't function without it. You will seek it out in future partners and when something healthy comes along that isn't based on those principles you may not recognize it because it doesn't fit into your expectations of what relationships are about.

If you've noticed this happening in your relationships there are things you can do. Talk to a counsellor or therapist firstly about how you're feeling and what is happening. You could also try writing down what attracts to you to certain people and see if you can identify any patterns from your childhood. When you are dating try to be open to meeting different kinds of people and get to know them first – it doesn't matter if it's not lust at first sight because, in time, something deeper will come.

Different expectations

When you start a relationship everything is rosy for a while and you have certain expectations. You project a fantasy image onto a partner, often putting them on a pedestal. You've finally met 'the one'. Subconsciously you're looking for someone who will 'save' you, bring excitement into your life and make you feel different, special and alive. You get caught up in the romance of it, and for some people, this is addictive. It's why so many of us have short-term flings – we prefer the thrill of the chase to the reality and hard work that goes into a long-term relationship.

After a while the blinkers come off and you start to notice things about your partner that niggle you. Once you scratch the surface you realize that, actually, your partner is exactly the same as you. The relationship is a mirror reflecting those things that you need to learn about yourself. If there are patterns or traits in your behaviour that you haven't learned how to deal with, you will keep attracting other people who share them until you do learn your lesson. This is when problems can start and the relationship hits rocky ground.

Try to acknowledge this behaviour in yourself and work out what your expectations are of a partner before you get involved. It helps to understand the lifecycle of a relationship and how long each stage lasts so that you aren't blinded by the initial lust and romance. We'll look at a typical relationship lifecycle later on (see page 60). It can also help to develop your own interests and personal space so that you aren't looking for a partner to fulfil all of your needs.

Money

Money is one of the biggest causes of stress between partners. If you've always saved and your partner spends willy-nilly with no regard for your future it will cause problems. Our attitudes towards money and debt are ingrained from an early age – how our parents managed money and whether it was an issue in the house and how responsible they taught you to be about it. You might not always be aware of conflicting values around money, especially at the start of a relationship but after a while they will become apparent.

As the story on page 45 shows, it's wise to keep an eye on joint finances and to be aware of how things are being handled. You can ask your bank/credit providers to keep you up-to-date with payment information.

Money can also cause a rift if it's used in the relationship to determine status. Do you argue about who brings in the money and who pays for things? Are you both happy with the arrangement? It can be hard if you suddenly experience a drop in income – like after having a baby and changing to part-time work. You may find that you prefer to keep your own finances separate and to have a joint bank account for household expenses. It's sensible to have a little nest egg of your own for your future security. It will give you peace of mind because you know that should anything happen later on you will be able to look after yourself.

Try to work out what your attitudes and patterns are around spending and saving. Talk to your partner about anything that concerns you. Go through your bank and credit card statements for the past six months and see if there is any excess spending. What areas can you both compromise on? Don't feel you have to stop enjoying your money. It is important to have little treats so keep some money aside for fun – for the two of you and for pampering things. You could both try keeping a daily spending diary to note any habits and compare notes at the end of each week. You'll be surprised at how much is frittered away on silly things.

If debt is an issue and you're splitting up because of it then call your local Citizens Advice Bureau (CAB) or the Consumer Credit Council – a free service, which rearranges your payments with creditors at a price you can afford each month (see Part 5, Chapters 15 and 16). Don't feel that you are trapped in a relationship because of money worries. There are always options for accommodation and negotiating your debts so take some advice if you need to.

Remember that there will never be enough money. Accepting that takes away any hold it has over you. It is a source of energy that flows in and out of our lives and to attract it we need to feel open, positive and relaxed about it.

I didn't realize how much debt we were in until the day the bailiffs turned up at our door. It turned out that my husband was months behind on payments and I knew nothing about it. I had a breakdown with all the stress. We had been married for over ten years and had children. We're now divorced and I live alone. It's definitely affected the way I handle money. I'm very careful not to overspend. I would never have a joint bank account or leave the financial arrangements to someone else again.

Sarah

Domestic violence

Being in an abusive relationship can destroy your confidence and self-esteem. People often take a dim view and will ask why you put up with it for so long, why you didn't leave earlier. However, it's not as easy as that. When you're in the thick of it you don't always realize how unacceptable a partner's behaviour is. Comments and actions can grind you down until you feel worthless and useless and then you daren't leave because 'no one else would have you'. You might be wondering if it's partly your fault and also feeling embarrassed and ashamed that it's happening and so you keep quiet about it. It can sometimes be easier to stay put and hope it will all go away especially when you're worried about how you'll manage financially on your own.

MYTH: Domestic violence only happens to women.

FACT: Domestic violence can happen to anyone. There has been a rise in the number of incidents towards men over the past few years. It can be mental or physical in nature and mental abuse can be more damaging because it's harder to prove.

Here are some examples of abusive behaviour. Think about whether any apply to your relationship. For example, does your partner:

- Threaten to hurt you or commit suicide if you go

- Make you do illegal things

- Intimidate you with a look or gesture

- Use weapons against you

- Inflict cruelty to animals in the house

- Put you down, calling you names or humiliating you

- Control what you do, who you see and how much money or work you have access to

- Say that it's your fault and that you deserve the abuse

- Threaten to take your children away from you if you go?
  (See **www.cri.org.uk**)

Facts about domestic violence:

- It is a serious issue and constitutes a quarter of all violent crime in the UK.
- It's often not reported to the police until an average of 35 incidents has taken place.
- It claims the lives of two women a week and 30 men per year.
- It will affect 1 in 4 women and 1 in 6 men in a lifetime.

(Information from **www.cri.org.uk**)

Deciding whether to stay or go

It's not always that simple to make a decision to stay or go. You may love your partner and no doubt, it's not all bad. You will have shared some happy times together. Perhaps the abuse only happens when he or she has had a few drinks and it's like they are a different person. They may be ashamed and embarrassed the next day or choose to ignore it and hope it will go away, which can be harder for you to deal with as you're not quite sure if you're overreacting.

Has your partner shown any remorse or offered to get help? Your doctor would be a good place to start. Talk to him or her about how you're feeling and if your partner is willing, get him or her to go along and see them too. Having someone to talk to about your feelings can help ease some of the pressure. There are special programmes men can join to help them work on their anger.

However ashamed you feel **don't bottle things up**. Talk to the police or Refuge if you can – they are trained to deal with these things and will take what you say very seriously. If you feel unsafe and need to find another place to live they will be able to help organize that, too.

Here are some things to organize if you're planning to leave:

- Write down any emergency telephone numbers and keep your phone charged.

- Keep copies and originals of any ID documents.

- Keep an extra set of keys in the house and car.

- Set money aside for emergencies.

- Keep a spare set of clothes for you and the children.

- Plan where you will go and be discreet about who you tell.

- Keep a diary of all incidents so that you have something to show the police and your doctor.

- Find out what will happen to your house if you decide to leave for a while. Can you get your partner to leave or get financial help?

- Think about getting some emotional support – counselling is an excellent place to start and will help to change your views and reactions to situations. You'll find a useful list of organizations in Part 5.

(See **www.cri.org.uk**)

My marriage failed because we weren't good together. We were both 23 and rushed into things and didn't have a long enough courtship period. It was a long-distance relationship as he lived in the States. We got married six months after he moved to the UK, as he would have been kicked out unless he got married or found a job. We did love each other but we didn't know each other well enough. The 'romance' covered up some inevitable problems – disrespect, jealousy, manipulation and a clash of backgrounds although I believed that we could work things out. He had anger management issues and wanted control of me constantly. There were violent rages that I couldn't control or deflate. Four days after our wedding blessing he screamed at me and left me on my own in a strange country late at night.

We had both gone for counselling and after talks with my parents I realized it was over and asked him for a divorce. It left me feeling scared and mentally bruised. I coped with it by drinking a lot and was in a high profile job so there was plenty of socializing. He tried to contact me and wouldn't agree to the divorce at first but he wasn't prepared to come over and try to work things out.

I worked myself to death and locked out certain friendships that were too demanding. To a degree I lost myself, something I've been working on to rediscover ever since. I got involved with unsuitable men and fell into lust with people who saw my vulnerability. I became a person that my friends didn't recognize. I had the same question running around in my head – how had I arrived at this point? Why would someone who married me treat me that way?

He was a great love and I enjoyed the romance of a long-distance relationship but it didn't work out practically. He was out of work most of the time that we were together so I was the breadwinner and I think he felt threatened by this. He was messy at home and I could never rely on him to do anything practically or emotionally.

It sounds awful in retrospect but it isn't all bad. I got out of a relationship with someone violent and my life is a much happier place now. I know what I want and how much I appreciate my current partner-in-crime. You need more than love for a successful relationship – you need cohesion and the willingness to work as a team, respect and give-and-take on a daily basis. You need to be at the same place of maturity in your lives. You have to realize what you have and treat the relationship like a precious egg. Relationships are great but they need as much work as a job and as much tenderness as a newborn child.

Deanna

Personal issues

When a partner has an issue with drinking, gambling or drugs it's as if there are three of you in the relationship already – and you are in third place. It can go hand in hand with domestic violence, as a partner who has an addiction may turn abusive. His or her behaviour won't be rational. He or she may lie to you and steal money from you or get into debt to fund the habit. You'll be feeling very stressed trying to hold things together – your job, the children, a roof over your head, your sanity. Sometimes you want to be a martyr – to cure him or her of addiction and, commendable as that is, it won't work unless your partner is committed to getting help. You may feel too embarrassed to tell anyone about it and it can feel like their addiction becomes your problem too, as you're checking up on him or her constantly and worrying about what will happen next.

Deciding whether to stay or go

Whether you decide to stay or go depends on how willing your partner is to face up to his or her demons and make some changes. You need to talk seriously about it, in a neutral setting if possible.

There are many organizations that can help and also many support organizations for you if you're struggling to cope, see Part 5 for details. Suggest that you go for counselling together and give your partner an ultimatum and a time limit for making changes. It shows that you mean what you say and that you will leave if nothing changes.

Infertility

You may have a sense of yourselves as parents and partners and when that possibility is removed it can put a huge strain on a relationship. The life you had planned out together isn't working. You probably both feel like you've failed and it's natural to look for someone or something to blame. You're both grieving for the loss of an unborn child and the continuation of your family. If you've paid for fertility treatment that hasn't worked there will also be added financial pressure. If there's no apparent physical reason for why you can't conceive then sex – rather than being a fun, relaxing activity – becomes a battleground.

You both need to take the pressure off each other. Spend some time away if you can, talking and reconnecting, and try to get a little perspective on the situation. It can be devastating but it's not the end of the world and you always have other options. It means you can both spend quality time together, pursue your careers and other interests, travel and lead interesting lives – probably much to the envy of your friends with children! Are there other options you could consider such as adoption? Consider how stressful your lives are right now and what changes you can make to relieve this.

It will help to speak to a professional organization such as Infertility Network UK, a charity that provides advice, support and information for people who are dealing with infertility. You can contact them on 08701 188 088 (further details in Part 5).

Stepfamilies

For many of you being in a stepfamily is a positive experience. Children have two families – and double the fun! However, not everyone feels that way initially. Some children find it very hard to accept that their mum or dad has a new partner and they may react by making your life very difficult. Parents sometimes dote on their children too much and feel so guilty about a break-up that they let them get away with murder and the new family unit suffers. As the new partner you may be seen as the 'evil' one who has split the family up and you may face a barrage of hostility and resentment for a while.

If this is the case and you're starting to wonder if it's worthwhile staying together then talk to your partner about how you're feeling. Try to give it some time – often these things will ride themselves out. Teenagers, in particular, can be moody creatures and they will go through sulky phases when they hate everyone and everything. Try not to take it personally as they are reacting to the situation not to you as a person. Create as welcoming a home as possible and make sure they know where you are if they do want to talk.

It's possible that you are feeling:

- Pushed out by your partner's family: 'You're not my real mum/dad and you can't tell me what to do!'

- Like you have no authority, command little respect and are trapped in the middle as your partner thinks butter wouldn't melt in his/her child's mouth.

- Unsure of your new role – are you a parent or a friend? How much should you discipline them?

- Jealous of your partner's ex and the history they share.

- Like you're walking on eggshells with them.

If you are experiencing difficulties here are a few suggestions that may help:

- Change your thinking. Life is too short to worry about it. Do everything you can to resolve the issue and if you can't then get some help through counselling. Call Parentline Plus – a free 24-hour helpline on 0808 800 2222.

- Talk to the children together about how their behaviour is making you both feel. It's more likely to be an issue if they are teens or older as their behaviour can be more manipulative. Know that it will pass.

- Arguments are healthy to a degree. Deal with each situation as it arises and then picture yourself putting it into a box and letting it go.

- Try to create routine in your family life. Sit down together for a meal every night and make space for talking. It doesn't matter if they choose to participate or not, they know that support is there when they need it.

- Ask them about their experiences of family life and explain yours.

- Try to find new activities that you like to do together.

- Don't try to be a replacement parent unless the children indicate that's what they want.

The lifecycle of a relationship

We are often asked how relationships change over time. If you're thinking about ending a relationship or have just finished one and aren't sure what went wrong it can help to understand the lifecycle of a relationship.

The first few weeks/early months are usually lust-driven (as a result of your hormones!). You may feel infatuated with your partner and unable to keep your hands off him or her. Sex is usually good and the relationship is quite physical. You find yourself thinking about your partner a lot.

The second stage can last from the first couple of months to around two years. You are seeing each other exclusively and are committed to the relationship. You may be living together and have noticed each other's bad habits. You're willing to compromise to make the relationship work.

In the third stage you move deeper into commitment – perhaps having children together or buying a house. At this point you're striving for your independence and space within the relationship. There may be times when you feel like being alone and pursuing your own interests.

In the final stages – you are relaxed within the relationship and know that you both can be yourselves. You set goals together and keep things moving. You're both developing as individuals within the relationship.

Deciding whether to stay or go

What else do you need to think about if you're deciding whether to stay or go? As you've been reading the first part of the book you've probably been applying things to your own relationship. If your partner has left you then you don't have a choice but you do have a choice in how you react and deal with it. If you're still mulling things over and aren't sure what you want here are a few things to consider. We've mentioned them already but it helps to have a concrete list at this point to remind you.

- Avoid making any rash decisions when you're upset or angry. You may regret leaving on impulse. Give it some time.

- Make sure that your decision is informed. Look at the relationship rather than blaming yourself or your partner for things that have gone wrong. What attracted you to each other in the first place? How has that changed? What do you love about him or her and what would you miss if things ended? What outside factors have influenced the relationship? Why can't you work things out?

- Write a list of pros and cons.

- Keep a diary of your feelings to help you work out what is really going on and what you want to do about it.

- Call a telephone counselling service such as Marriage Care or Relateline (see Part 5, Chapter 15) for an independent view.

- Think about how balanced your life is within the relationship. Does it fulfil your needs? Draw a large circle on a piece of paper and divide it into sections – Health, Relationships, Sex, Work/Money and Leisure – depending how much prominence each area has in your relationship. Is any area out of balance?

- Go to see your doctor for a check-up. If you're run down then you may be feeling miserable and your relationship will suffer without you knowing why.

Visualization exercise – with or without?

Take ten minutes to do a visualization exercise. It will help to put you in touch with your intuition to make the right decision. Imagine life without your partner. What is it like? What are you doing? How do you feel? A few hours later do the same experience again, this time imagining life with your partner. Do you notice any differences in how you feel on each occasion? Does one option make you feel happy or full of dread? Don't think too hard about it – the aim is to help you tap into your instincts.

Trial separation

Is it possible to negotiate a trial separation and how does it work? A trial separation can be a good way to get some perspective on the situation without making any instant decisions. It gives you both space and time to think about things, to decide what's important and what's not. You can use the time to go through the checklist on pages 61–2 and set your boundaries if you feel you need to. You can also test the water a bit – pursue life as a singleton again, hook up with old friends and make an effort to meet new people. It also gives you time to get some professional advice on where you stand legally if you are to split.

How to negotiate a trial separation

- Set a time limit to meet up and talk about things. Keep it businesslike and avoid going over old ground. The point is to think about the future and how you can make things work.

- Meet on neutral ground rather than at home.

- Set some clear guidelines – who will stay in the house and who will go? If you're leaving, where will you go?

- Tell your friends and family what you're planning to do.

- Discuss how you'll handle the children

- Think about where your relationship is now in terms of the relationship lifecycle. Where do you need more support? What do you want from a relationship now? How have things changed since you met? What do you both hope to achieve from the time apart?

- Once the trial separation has started don't contact your partner, unless necessary for children.

If you've had some time apart and have both decided you'd like to make another go of things then accept that the old relationship has gone and something new is about to begin. That means new ground rules and respect for one another. Make a list of who will do what to improve certain areas. Review it after a month to see if things have improved. Have your priorities changed? What is important to you both now? You don't have to go back to things as they were before. If you can't live with your partner's messy habits, for example, think about ways around it. Can you negotiate your own space within the house? Some couples 'live apart together' – they live independently in their own accommodation during the week and spend quality time together at the weekends. It's one way of injecting a bit of romance – if you can afford it!

If the relationship has broken down and you want to move on then you'll need to think about the practicalities. Our checklists in Chapter 4 will help you to organize things. If you are amicable and can talk face to face then do so. Your partner deserves your respect and he or she is more likely to accept what you are saying if it's face to face rather than by phone, letter or via someone else. Tell a friend what you're planning to do so that they are on standby should you need some support.

3

Your survival guide –
month 1

The final section of Part 1 is an emotional and practical survival guide to help you get through the first month. It explains what to expect in the first few days and weeks and how your feelings will change. The first month can be very hard as you're trying to work out what has happened as well as dealing with the immediate grief and everyone else's reactions. In the next part of the book we'll guide you through the first year and explain how to deal with recurrent emotions that you might be finding difficult to deal with.

In her seminal book, *On Death and Dying*, psychiatrist Elizabeth Kubler-Ross identified that there are five stages of coping with grief and loss. It's normal to go through these in any order:

- Denial

- Resentment

- Bargaining

- Depression

- Acceptance.

MYTH: *Men get over break-ups much more quickly than women do.*

FACT: Not true. Men take break-ups just as hard as women do and, in some cases, find them harder to overcome because they may not have the same support networks. They may choose to keep their feelings to themselves, believing that it's not the done thing to talk about everything and that they should be in control. This can make it harder to move on.

Day 1

Expect the first couple of days to be the worst and take comfort in knowing that you'll feel a lot better soon. You might be reeling from the shock if it was unexpected, feeling guilty if you've decided to leave, or be on autopilot, going through the motions, because if you stop to think about things for a minute you'll fall to pieces. You're probably obsessing over what went wrong, feeling angry about the way you've been treated, or longing for a second chance to put things right. **Remember that you are not alone.**

- Go with your feelings. Cry it out. Rant and rave. Grieve for what has gone and give yourself some space and time.

- If you're feeling angry do something physical to help you release it – try a kick-boxing class, go for a run, drive somewhere quiet and yell until you're hoarse, or write a letter to your ex explaining how you feel but don't post it.

- Be alone if you want to.

- If you're feeling numb listen to some uplifting music or watch a sad film to help you to get in touch with your emotions. Sometimes it's a case of giving yourself permission to let go.

- Call a friend and explain what's happened. Ask for support if you need it.

- Write your feelings down on paper. Get them out of your head and then burn the paper without re-reading.

- Start a diary and write down how you're feeling each day.

- Look after yourself. Take a warm bath, eat something simple, go for a walk, and nap when you need to. Exercise raises your serotonin levels and will make you feel more positive and able to cope.

- Breathe deeply for ten minutes. This will help if you're feeling panicky.

- Don't contact your partner.

- Don't make any important decisions today.

Survival tips

- Look after yourself

- Give yourself time to grieve

- Start to move on.

Week 1

On the second and third days you'll probably be feeling a bit more resigned. The initial panic will go and you will start to think a little more rationally about the next steps. Money may be tight right now and you may need to watch your spending. This will change as you get back into your routines and things settle down. For now, things like cooking from scratch will be a lot cheaper and healthier than relying on ready meals. Try to make some small changes in your lifestyle to help your budget. Next:

- Think about the practicalities – spring clean and get rid of anything belonging to your ex. Put it in a box in the garage for him or her to collect or throw it away and reclaim the space as yours. Take down any photos. Buy some new bed linen.

- Get your diary out and make a few plans with friends. Call those you haven't been in touch with lately and arrange to meet up. Make sure you have plans for the next few weekends. It doesn't have to involve eating and drinking out – you can meet up at a friend's house for a coffee.

- Think about and write down your thoughts and feelings around what went wrong and your part in it. Try to be dispassionate about where the fault lies. Owning up to your mistakes is powerful – it gives you a sense of control and means you can choose to do things differently next time around.

- Make sure you get out and do some exercise at least three times this week. Don't overdo it though – take it easy to begin with. A half hour walk is fine. Dancing is a great way to release pent-up emotions – try the '5 Rhythms' – a powerful movement practice devised by Gabrielle Roth in the sixties. You can find classes nationwide. Perhaps you can walk or

bike to work or town rather than taking the
car, if you have one.

- Take a long bath and have a complete pamper
  – hands, feet, hair and nails. Wear something
  you feel great in.

- Write a list of the things you used to love to
  do when you were single and plan to do a few
  over the next few weeks.

- Get some legal advice over the house and your
  rights. It might be painful to go through
  everything with a stranger right now but you
  may come to regret it if you let things go.

- Make an appointment to talk to a counsellor if
  you want to talk things through.

- Make sure you do at least one thing a day that
  lifts your spirits – be it going for a walk,
  talking to a friend or reading the paper. Try to
  keep in touch with the outside world.

Weeks 2–4

During weeks 2–4:

- Keep up your routines – go out with friends, start a new course, keep exercising, do a bit of shopping to lift your spirits and congratulate yourself on getting through the first week.

- Spend some quality time with yourself. If there's something you've always wanted to do, such as ride a horse or go skydiving, do your research and when you can afford it, book it.

- Write down your longer-term plans – what do you really want to achieve in your life? Are you happy at work? Do you want to start a business? What gets you fired up?

- Plan a break with your friends.

- Appreciate that you'll have good days and bad days. Grieving isn't a straightforward process.

- Give a friend or family member a key to your house so that you can arrange to have someone to come home to in the evenings.

- Contact your local Adult Education college and book yourself in for an image consultation and a beauty treatment or haircut. Fashion and beauty students always need willing volunteers and it won't cost you much. Most department stores offer free makeovers and beauty samples too.

Keep an eye out for depression. There are two main types:

- **Reactive**. This occurs when life has been affected by illness, bereavement or divorce, job loss or financial disaster.

- **Endogenous**. This comes upon you out of the blue. There may be a family history of depression. Occasionally, the sufferer will experience mood swings, from despair to high spirits and back again.

Reactive is the most common after a divorce or break-up. Endogenous can creep up on you out of the blue and you might swing between feeling high and low. It can also make you feel negative about your relationships. Quite often we don't even realize that we're depressed until someone else points it out.

Here are some signs of depression. Tick any that apply:

❏ Poor appetite

❏ Difficulty sleeping

❏ Loss of energy

❏ Poor concentration

❏ Feeling guilty

❏ Loss of libido

❏ Avoiding social activities and contact

❏ Thinking about suicide or dying.

How did you do? If you're experiencing five of these it's a good idea to see your doctor. Contact one of the support organizations listed in Part 5, Chapter 15. Depression is easily treated with psychological support and anti-depressants.

4

Practical lifelines

In the final chapter of Part 1 we're going to look at all the practicalities you need to consider over the next few months. Think of this as your daily checklist and pull it out and stick it to the fridge if need be. It will help to guide you through the various stages of divorce or separation. It's very difficult to remember what you need to do when you're feeling emotional and upset so make sure you get professional advice if you're unsure about anything. If you can, obtain advice from a solicitor before the break-up regarding your position on the house and your finances so that you know where you stand. Contacting a solicitor for advice will be helpful – it doesn't mean that you are committed to using them in the long term or that you have to get a divorce. You can take it as far as you want and no further.

Your finances

Breaking up can be expensive. It's also stressful because it can take a long time to finalize settlements, during which time you've got to eat, live and support yourself as normal. You might have the extra cost of renting a new home if you've left the shared house. You might have children to raise on your own if your partner has left and you are waiting for maintenance to come through. It can be a very trying and worrying time. Avoid the temptation to live off your credit cards and if debt is an issue contact the Citizens Advice Bureau (CAB) or Consumer Credit Counselling Service (CCCS). They will work out your budget and renegotiate payments with your creditors at a price you can afford to pay each month. Debt can be debilitating so talking to someone about it and having a plan of action will help you to feel more positive. Generally speaking people who are separating either do it

---

MYTH: Most people get into debt through over-spending.

FACT: Relationship breakdown contributes to over half of all debt problems.

properly and cut all financial ties or will bury their heads in the sand and hope everything sorts itself out. The first approach is the most advisable! It's tempting to try to do things amicably, and avoid stress and divorce lawyers, but you may regret this later on if you lose out financially.

There are a few essentials you need to organize if you or your partner are leaving the home. Stick a list on the fridge so you don't forget!

Home and finances

The first thing you should do is to take independent financial advice to consider how things are now and to get a longer-term plan. You will need to create a little nest egg for your future security if you don't already have one in place. A financial adviser will be able to advise on mortgages, pensions, savings and debt.

- If you're leaving the house take legal advice from your solicitor or CAB so you know where you stand. If your financial situation is complicated, a divorce lawyer will be able to establish what you're entitled to.

- Plan your new budget. Write a list of all your monthly outgoings and who is responsible for the bills. Ask your bank for a recent statement and a list of your direct debits and standing orders as there may be things you need to cancel.

- Do you need help with bills? Can you ask friends or family for a short-term loan? If debt is an issue, speak to your creditors and advise them on the situation, as you may be able to negotiate repayments at a reduced rate for the next few months. Contact the Consumer Credit Counselling Service (CCCS) or the National Debtline (see Part 5 for details) for advice on debt.

- Write down a list of things to discuss with your partner and agree a time to talk. You'll need to think about the house, car, children, debts and finances, any pets and your shared possessions. It's important to keep up repayments on the house or you may be left with a bad credit rating or face eviction.

- Settle any outstanding bills or debts if you can. Take meter readings and copies of bills. Ask for your or your partner's name to be removed from the bills depending on who is staying in

the property. Ask for final bills to be sent to
the new address.

- Do you own or are you renting? If renting, can
  you change your tenancy type so that you are
  the sole tenant? If you own jointly can you buy
  your partner out or vice versa?

- Get advice on your mortgage if you have one –
  are there any attached investments you need
  to organize?

- Apply for legal aid immediately if you need it
  – it may take a while to come through.

- Contact the council and enquire about any
  benefits you may be entitled to, such as
  reduction in council tax for sole occupier or
  tax credits.

- Notify your bank of any changes. If you have a
  joint account, can you withdraw your money
  and cancel the account? If your partner has
  access to other accounts you may need to
  change them.

- Get a copy of your credit report from Experian
  (**www.experian.co.uk**) or Equifax
  (**www.equifax.co.uk**) so you can see if there
  are any debts in your name.

- If you feel daunted by money and don't understand how things work consider doing a class at your local college in basic bookkeeping or accounting. This will help you feel more in control of your finances. You can run the household expenses on your computer, which takes a lot of the stress out of things.

- Do some reading to improve your knowledge – there are lots of good books about how finances work.

- Get organized and have a filing system for your bills and statements.

- Use internet money websites to help you budget and learn about finances. They will also have information about the best savings rates, credit cards and mortgages.

- Switch your credit cards to a low or zero interest account if you can.

- If you are divorcing you might not be able to make changes to joint bank accounts or credit cards. You are liable for any debts incurred in both your names so try to come to an agreement early on about how debts will be organized.

*I think the financial stuff should come
before the emotional stuff in a way
because if your finances go wrong it can
take years to recover, especially if you
end up going to court. It can stop you
moving on. My partner owed me a lot of
money in the end and despite his
promises to pay me back I haven't seen
a penny of it yet!*

Anna

- Notify your doctor, dentist and school of your new address or change in circumstances. Your doctor may be able to refer you to other organizations for help. It's also a good idea to have a general health check.

- Notify your boss in case you can't get in to work immediately. Deal with any urgent matters if you can and let work know a date for your return or organize time off if you need to. Inform the accounts department as your tax code might have changed. If you feel nervous about calling and aren't feeling organized, prepare a list of things to say and have your wage slips handy when you call.

- Decide what to do about the computer if you have one. You may want to change passwords for online banking or email accounts. You may be able to transfer your Internet Service Provider (ISP) to a new address.

- Redirect your mail. You can do this for a minimum of one month but make sure you organize it a couple of weeks before you move out as it can take a while to set up.

- Cancel or bar any 'second' mobile phone accounts.

- If your partner has changed the locks call the CAB or your local council for advice – their housing/tenancy relations office can advise you on your rights. If you own the home jointly your partner has to allow you access. If you are renting it depends on the type of tenancy agreement you have. If your partner won't allow you access you may need to get a solicitor to write to him or her, or you can ask the court for an Order to enter. If you find yourself evicted by your partner and are homeless call Shelter (see Part 5, Chapter 15) or your local council – they can organize emergency accommodation for you.

- If your partner is being violent or unreasonable contact the police.

- You probably won't be able to take all of your belongings at once so pack up the most important things – any bills, medical or legal documents and useful telephone numbers, your diary, purse, cash or credit cards and any valuables, your keys, mobile phone and charger, driving licence, any medication and your computer. Take a couple of changes of clothes for you and the children – and something smart if you're going to work.

- If your partner is leaving the house get the keys back.

- You might need boxes and cleaning equipment to pack stuff up. Put your stuff into storage if you need to.

Children

- Talk to the children together beforehand so they know what to expect.

- Pack a bag for the children ahead of time if you can. A change of clothing, favourite toys, medication, medical notes, school contact details.

Friends and family

- Call a close friend or family member to help out. Explain what is happening and ask for help with accommodation or finances beforehand if you can.

- Keep a notebook in your bag to note down any questions, conversations and thoughts so you can keep track of things you need to do over the next few weeks. It might be helpful to have a copy of any verbal 'agreement' you've made with your ex-partner regarding your house and property.

Divorce or separation?

Divorce

Divorce is the final step – a formal termination of the marriage – so you both need to be sure it's what you really want. You will have considered your options, spoken to friends and family and taken some professional advice. To apply for a divorce in England and Wales you need to have been married for at least a year. If you were married abroad you need to have been living here in the UK for one year before divorcing.

To apply for a divorce, you will need to cite one of the following:

- Adultery

- Unreasonable behaviour

- Desertion

- Two years separated if you both agree

- Five years separated.

You can contact a solicitor to initiate proceedings or you can do it yourself. The latter isn't advisable unless your situation is very simple. The evidence you give is set out in a document called a Petition for Divorce.

What next?

If your partner accepts the divorce he or she tells the court and you'll be kept informed. You will also be told if your partner doesn't want to go ahead. If it's a fairly simple situation you'll be sent a form telling you when the judge will grant your divorce. There are two stages of divorce: decree nisi, given by the court when they are satisfied that grounds have been reached, and decree absolute, which is the final stage.

In simple cases, it can take as little as four to six weeks from filling in the form to the final stage. It will take much longer if the situation is complex and there are children involved. Your solicitor will be able to advise.

Online/DIY divorce

You can apply online via websites if things are relatively straightforward. Your local court will also have a do-it-yourself divorce pack. However, this isn't advisable if you have shared property, financial issues or children.

Separation

There is no such thing as 'common law' marriage in the UK. If you aren't married then there are no legal ties to bind. This also applies to those of you who are living with a partner. If you aren't married then the courts can't issue an instruction to transfer property or assets. This is something to be aware of if you are cohabiting – but you can sign a cohabiting agreement to determine what happens to the house should you split. Not exactly romantic, but very sensible!

If you intend to divorce later on then you could consider formally separating. You will need to make a note of any arrangements regarding children, property and finances in a legal document called a 'deed of separation'. This sets out what you've agreed to do.

If you or your partner are religious and wish to separate but don't want to divorce you can opt for a Judicial Separation. You will have to prove grounds for the separation. It means that the courts can decide what to do about property and finances.

Mediation

This can be helpful if you're splitting up and can't agree on things. A mediator is present to help you talk openly about how to reach a settlement about property, money and children. However, it's not a substitute for legal advice so talk to your solicitor first. Be aware that amicable agreements can backfire later on. You can get free legal advice from CLS Direct (**www.clsdirect.org.uk**).

Q. How do we divide our possessions?

A. You'll need legal advice on how to split property, cars and money. With regard to your personal possessions it's very much down to the two of you to decide who gets what. Try to share goods equally and fairly, according to who paid for what or who is paying for goods if they are on credit. It can help to make a list so you can divide things equally.

Wills

It's advisable to make a will even if you don't have huge amounts of money or assets. When you die there are rules governing what happens to your property and possessions so it's a way of ensuring things are distributed as you would like. If you already have a will and are separated and your ex-partner is with someone else then you may want to change it. You can draw up a will yourself if it's likely to be straightforward although it's advisable to get a solicitor to check the final copy. Think about the following before you take legal advice to reduce costs:

- How much money do you have? What are your assets in terms of property, possessions, insurance policies and a pension?

- Who would you like to give your money to?

- Who will look after any children under 18?

- Who would you like to execute your wishes?

Organizing a pension

If you don't have a pension in place then speak to the CAB or an independent financial adviser about which type to take out. It's comforting to know that you do have some security for your retirement. There are several types:

- **Basic state pension** – a fixed rate that you get on retirement if you've paid enough National Insurance contributions during your life.

- **Additional pension** – a top-up that is based on your actual earnings. If you are an employee you have to contribute unless you join a personal pension scheme, which is contracted out.

- **Occupational** – this is set up by your employers to provide a pension and extra benefits.

- **Personal** – you can take out a personal pension regardless of whether you are employed, self-employed or unemployed.

Contact The Pensions Advisory Service (TPAS) if you'd like more advice (**www.pensionsadvisory service.org.uk**).

Organizing tax and benefits

If you split up you will be treated as individuals by the tax office so any benefits you are receiving will change. You need to tell them about your new circumstances, as you may be eligible for new benefits. For example, if you are paying maintenance you may be entitled to limited income tax relief. If you're on a low income you might be entitled to claim the following:

- Child support
- Children's tax credit
- Council tax benefit
- Grant towards cost of home repairs
- Housing benefit
- Income support
- Jobseeker's allowance
- Social fund
- Working tax credit.

You can find out what you might be entitled to on the Department for Work and Pensions website – **www.dwp.gov.uk**.

Children, friends and extended family

Explain what has happened and try to be calm and rational. Avoid bad-mouthing your partner. Try to avoid arguing in front of the children and keep them informed of your plans. It's important that they understand that the break-up is in no way their fault. Make sure they see their grandparents regularly to maintain routine. Your parents and in-laws might be worried that they won't be able to see the children so reassure them that this isn't the case and things will continue as normal.

You are both equally responsible for your children regardless of whom they live with, and the main carer is entitled to child support from the non-resident partner. It's also a good idea to tell their school what is happening as the split may cause some disruption.

*Find a very understanding friend or ask
a sibling to help you. It needs to be
someone that you trust and who will
take over while you're on autopilot. He
or she needs to be able to take over
everything from making sure you eat
properly, to getting you up at a normal
time and even washing your hair! They
can collect your belongings and post and
take you out for walks and cups of tea.
In other words, someone who will be a
mother to you for a while.*

Laura

Child maintenance

This is paid by the non-resident parent to help with childcare costs. The Child Support Agency (CSA) currently organizes it.* It should be noted that the CSA only applies to biological and adoptive children. If you are separating from your children's step-parent, the CSA will not apply to this person and you will have to claim maintenance through another provision and should see a lawyer. The amount you will get depends on your partner's income after tax and the number of children involved. You can apply online and use a 'calculation checker' to see how much you're likely to receive. It doesn't affect your tax credits. The CSA has the power to take action if your partner refuses to pay. As a rough guideline, a non-resident parent is required to pay 15 per cent of their net income for one child, 20 per cent for two and 25 per cent for three or more.

You won't be entitled to any child maintenance if your partner:

*At the time of writing, the CSA is being disbanded and replaced by a new body called the Child Maintenance and Enforcement Commission. This will be introduced over the next few years and will have a much tougher policy on the collection and enforcement of child maintenance. In the meantime, cases will be assessed as normal via the CSA.

- Is in prison

- Is a student in full-time education

- Lives outside of the UK, unless he or she is working for a UK-based company.

The CSA is not the only way of dealing with child maintenance, you might instead want to discuss this as part of your financial arrangements on divorce.

Your home

Short-term options

Decide who is staying and who is moving out or how you'll manage things if you both have to stay in the same house for a while. If you do have to stay in the same house, set boundaries and have separate rooms if at all possible. Perhaps you can you stay with friends or family while you sort yourself out. **Always get legal advice** before you leave the home, even if it's just in the short term. Contact your local CAB or Shelter for advice on your rights. Always keep a spare set of house keys so you have access.

If the situation is violent and you need to

leave, contact Women's Aid, Refuge, the Men's Advice Line or your local council. You can apply for homelessness via the council and will get help to find temporary housing. Be aware that if you have a joint-tenancy agreement on a flat the council may not accept your application immediately because you're not 'homeless' in legal terms.

Longer-term options

Council housing is allocated on a points-based system. How quickly you are offered somewhere depends on a number of factors: how long you've been on the waiting list, your current housing situation, whether you have children, and medical and welfare grounds. If you have had medical support for depression or breakdown following your break-up declare it on your application form to help speed the process up.

Remember that you'll also need to get your mail redirected to your new address.

Private rentals

This is the quickest option if you are in a financial position to do so. You will need to pay a deposit and a month's rent in advance. There may also be admin fees for the agency. You will be asked for references and there will be a credit check. However, this may be dropped if you're able to pay some money upfront to secure the let.

Buying your home

If you're thinking about buying your house or buying your partner's share in it take some legal advice first. If you're applying for a mortgage go to the main lenders or you may pay more interest. If your partner is living in the house after you've left and refusing to pay the mortgage make sure the lenders are informed – if it's in joint names **you are both liable for any debts** incurred.

Consider what may happen if you decide to leave or if you want to return to the house later on. If your partner owns the house and wishes to sell make sure the settlement is fair and you get what you are entitled to. If your partner is still living in the house, again, make sure that you get paid for your share in it.

Tenancy

This very much depends on the type of tenancy you have. If it's a sole tenancy in your name it will end according to the terms you agreed (usually one year). If you and your partner share the tenancy you will need to let your landlord know if he or she is leaving or you may both be asked to leave. You can ask for it to be transferred to your name if you wish to keep the tenancy on and think about finding someone new to help with the rent.

Whatever your situation seek some legal advice so you know where you stand. If your partner is being difficult and refusing to let you into the home or has changed the locks, you do have rights regardless of whether you own or rent your home. You may be able to apply for an occupation order through the courts to give you access.

My wife refused to sell the house so in the end I had to force her out by getting a solicitor involved. It turned out she hadn't been paying the mortgage for months and had deceived me about our financial status as well as other things. The first I knew about it was when the bailiffs turned up at our door. We split the house 50/50 in the end. I could have gone for more but it would have meant an expensive legal battle and I knew she had no money so there seemed little point. I took the furniture as it was on credit in my name and I was paying it off over three years. I didn't see why she should get the benefit of that!

Things weren't straightforward. She stayed in the house and refused to pay the mortgage so the bank sent letters of repossession to me as it was in joint names. I explained that I was no longer living there and that the house was up for sale. If we didn't sell it would be repossessed and we'd both lose out, as they would flog it cheaply for a quick sale. I kept the dog as I'd paid for him and I knew she wouldn't take care of him.

My lowest point came when I lost my job shortly afterwards. I had rent and bills to pay. It was the first time I'd ever applied for benefits and I couldn't get anything at first because they wanted to see letters proving that the house had been sold. I was depressed and suicidal and had a nervous breakdown with the stress. The job had been physically demanding and I felt exhausted. It took a while but I got some benefits and was given a place to stay by the council.

Owen

Q. What about pets?

A. Who bought the pet? What are your lifestyles like? Who has more time to care for it? Pets can often cause arguments because there is emotional attachment on both sides and it can sometimes signify the loss of the relationship itself. Animal charities will help with the re-housing of pets if your circumstances have changed and you are no longer able to care for a pet. See Part 5 for a list of organizations that can help.

Custody of the children

This is likely to be the most challenging and emotional part of your break-up. You will both want to do what is best for your children and this can cause tension and arguments. The children will be hugely affected by the split, regardless of how well they seem to be coping outwardly, so it's important to try and deal with things professionally and calmly. Avoid using the children as pawns between the two of you. Try not to criticize your partner in front of them and don't make the children feel pressured into taking sides or making decisions that they are not ready to face.

Try to put your own feelings aside and, if you can, come to an amicable arrangement regarding the children's welfare. Decide between you who will look after them and how often they will see the other parent. Try to plan ahead, especially around times such as Christmas and holidays. You are both financially responsible for the children after a break-up, it doesn't matter where the children are living or whether you are married or not.

If the split is amicable and you've come to an agreement over financial support and housing arrangements then you can fill in a form called a "Statement of Arrangements" (SOA) without going to court. This sets things out formally – where the children live and with whom, where they go to school and when they will have contact with the non-resident parent – so you have a record, and you'll both need to sign it. You can get these forms from a county divorce court or download them online.

If you and your partner are having difficulty agreeing what to do about the children you can arrange for family mediation, which means that an independent person will help you to decide. You need to make sure that your childcare arrangements are satisfactory, otherwise the court may not agree to the divorce. If relations are fraught and you aren't in contact, get some legal advice. As a last resort you can approach the courts for help, although this can be an expensive and time-consuming process. The courts can decide who a child should live with (Residence Order), who the child sees and what kind of contact it will be (Contact Order), and whether the father should have parental responsibility, if he doesn't already have it (Parental Responsibility Order).

'Parental responsibility' means that you are responsible for a child's welfare. If you are

married, you both share it. If you are unmarried,
the mother has an automatic right to look after a
child. If you were not married when the child was
born then a father only has parental responsibility
if:

- He jointly signed the birth certificate, after
  1 December 2003

- You have signed a formal Parental
  Responsibility Agreement (you can do this at
  any time during the relationship or after the
  break-up)

- The courts have given the father parental
  responsibility

- The father is legal guardian of the children.

You are both jointly responsible for supporting a
child financially. It is good if you can make a
decision about child support and maintenance
yourselves, as a voluntary agreement, although it
is probably best to get legal advice to make sure
the amount and frequency of payments is fair. A
solicitor will be able to draw up an agreement that
sets things out clearly to avoid any future
problems.

Q: How do I find a good solicitor?

A: Finding a good solicitor is very important. He or she is there to offer you practical and legal advice and you need to feel comfortable and supported. However, it's worth remembering that he or she isn't there to be your therapist – there are other people you can turn to for emotional help such as Marriage Care or Relate. Ask friends and family for a recommendation and go to see a few solicitors before making your final choice. Most firms will offer a free consultation over the phone or face to face, which can be helpful in making a decision. Don't feel pressured into doing anything until you are ready and don't be afraid to change your solicitor if things aren't working out. If you're divorcing and need a solicitor, The Divorce Bureau (0800 731 9831) can find you a local solicitor.

We've covered a lot of ground in this section so take some time to think about what you need to do next. If you're unsure about your rights it's always best to get some legal advice, no matter how trivial it might seem. Talk to friends and family, too, if you can, as they will have experiences you can draw from. There is a lot to take on board and it's not easy to sort out practicalities when you're feeling emotional and run down. Try to take things one day at a time and remember to look after yourself.

In the next part we'll look at how you're feeling now the immediate crisis has passed and how you can begin to create a new identity for yourself. We'll suggest how to rebuild your existing relationships as well as develop new ones. There's a lot to look forward to so take a break now and do something nice for yourself.

Part 2:
Taking the Next Steps, Taking Control

In the first part of the book we looked at common reasons for relationship breakdown and the lifecycle of a relationship. We encouraged you to grieve for what has gone and suggested some practical, immediate things you could do to help. The next section is all about taking positive action to move forward. It's about having a little fun again and getting to know yourself. The emphasis is on *you* – healing yourself physically and mentally so that you feel stronger and more able to cope with the reactions of those around you. At times, it might feel like you are public property and that everyone has an opinion on how you should run your life. We want to encourage you to take stock and work out where you are right now and where you would like to be in the future. Hopefully, by the end of this part you'll be feeling energized, positive and optimistic about what lies ahead. It might be the end of your life as you know it but it's also the beginning of a new and exciting time when you can make your dreams a reality.

5

Emotional lifelines

In this chapter we're going to look at how you're feeling now the first few weeks have passed and also how those closest to you will be feeling about the break-up. If you haven't told everyone yet, we've got a few suggestions about how to go about it and what reactions to expect.

Your feelings

So how are you feeling right now? Has anything changed? Here are some common reactions to a break-up:

- You are in denial – you don't want to accept it.

- You are fearful – you're afraid to face life on your own again.

- You are learning to adapt – you're trying to strike a balance between giving and taking now that things have changed.

- You are lonely – you may be feeling desperately lonely or, alternatively, you may be coming to terms with it.

- You feel withdrawn – from your friends and family.

- You feel guilty or neglected – depending on whether you are the dumper or the dumpee.

- You are grieving – for the person and life you had.

- You are angry – at being rejected and lied to.

- You have low self-esteem – you have taken a big knock and this may affect the way you deal with the break-up.

- You feel to blame – whether you are the cause of the break-up or whether you suggested the split because of something your partner did.

Whatever your feelings it's important to acknowledge them to move on. Try making a list of your feelings right now – about your ex-partner, the relationship, what you have learned from it – so that you have something to reflect on later on when you're looking back on the relationship.

The first few weeks after a break-up are incredibly stressful. Some days will be bearable, others you'd rather forget about. It might feel like you're moving one step forward and two steps back. Hopefully not seeing your partner on a daily basis has given you some time and space to consider the relationship and you're starting to feel a little more in control. You might still be obsessing or worrying about things – unanswered questions, replaying moments or telling yourself 'if only'. That's fine. Don't beat yourself up, as it's normal to feel that way. You might be itching to get back out there and meet new people but are a little nervous because it's been a while. Or, perhaps you're hoping your ex will see the error of his or her ways and come back to you.

How to deal with days when you think 'I just can't go on...'

If you've hit rock bottom and feel like you don't have the strength or will to go on then please talk to someone and get some professional help. Don't keep it all inside. It's too much for you to bear on your own and you will feel much better if you share your feelings. Call one of the support organizations such as Marriage Care (0207 371 1341) or Careline (0845 122 8622). Both offer an advice/counselling service. If you've got other worries to contend with such as debt or family issues it can be overwhelming – your doctor or a telephone counselling service.

- Don't try to cope with your feelings on your own, you will feel much better once you talk to someone independent.

- You've already made a positive start to dealing with your feelings by reading this book.

Handling other people

This can be daunting, particularly if the break-up is acrimonious and you've got to face people on your own. People are unpredictable and it might feel like your relationship has suddenly become public property. Everyone wants a piece of you and it may feel like you've got to justify your behaviour and meet their approval. They might want to know every little detail when, in fact, you don't really feel like discussing it at all. Here are a few suggestions on how to handle those closest to you.

Your friends and family

How and when you choose to tell them will make a difference in how well they handle it. Choose the right time – you may want to wait a few days if there is something important going on in the family. If you can, talk to them together with your partner so that they can see that it's a mutual, considered decision. They are more likely to accept it is final if you both tell them together, face to face. They won't be able to blame either of you if you are both there to answer questions. Reassure the in-laws that they won't lose contact with their grandchildren. Talk to one or two close friends about how you're feeling. It can help to have more than one person to lean on so that you aren't putting too much pressure on certain people or expecting too much.

Grief – It's as much a break-up for them as it is for the two of you so give them time to adjust. Your parents may be worried about not seeing your children or that one of you will try to make things difficult. They might also be feeling guilty about whether they have contributed to it – especially if they are no longer together themselves.

Divided loyalties – Your mutual friends might be worried about losing your friendship. They may feel torn and think that they have to take sides. Your in-laws will be protective and loyal towards your partner but they may feel torn because they are emotionally attached to you as well. They may feel angry to be in this position and accuse you of being selfish. They may try to make you feel guilty, particularly if children are involved, wanting things to go back to how they were. Some of your friends may fall away and others will become closer.

Denial – They are hoping that you'll both see sense and get back together. They might think that it's a temporary phase and refuse to accept what you're saying. This could go on for a while until they accept the situation. They may try to think of ways to reconcile you in the meantime.

Hostility – 'Oh, he was no good for you anyway.' Or, 'I always thought she was selfish.' Sometimes people say these things without thinking about the consequences. They may try to knock your ex-partner down to protect you. Try not to moan about your ex – it will only make you feel bitter and unable to move on. Friends and family might make it seem as if the entire relationship was a waste of time but that isn't true. You were happy initially, and you have learned things about yourself from being with your partner. In a worst-case scenario they may cut you off completely and that is devastating because it's double the loss. Perhaps they struggled with their own relationship but stuck it out and put on a brave face because that's what people did. Divorce wasn't an option then. Well, times have changed and you don't have to stay in an unhappy relationship for the sake of saving face.

Being overbearing – They may charge in and want to run the show, wanting to know all the details about why it happened or they might be too sympathetic which can feel overbearing. When they do finally accept that it's over – and it can take some time – they may feel sad and depressed for you and also for what they have lost. Over time this should pass and they will be supportive.

Here are some suggestions for handling tricky conversations:

- Plan what you're going to say and come straight out with it. Be kind and tactful but there's no need to give them full details.

- Talk to your closest friends and family first so that you have some support before tackling the more challenging family members.

- Do it together if you can. Tell them what efforts you have both made to save the relationship and why it is over. If the split is acrimonious then tell them on your own to avoid arguments.

- Be strong and don't let them push you around. You've made your decision so stick to it. Don't feel guilty or selfish. It would be far more irresponsible to stay in an unhappy relationship for the 'sake of the children'.

- Give them time to accept what you're saying and create a bit of distance if you need to.

Your ex-partner

This depends on the circumstances of the split but even if your ex ended it there will still be a little sadness that things didn't work out. Your partner will be thinking and processing what went wrong, much as you are, and wondering about his/her part in it. He/she will be feeling upset, exhausted and a bit lonely, too, wondering what the future will bring. If the split was mutual and amicable then he/she is probably hoping you will stay in touch.

Your children

If you have children the impact on them will be significant and how they react depends on their age and maturity. Younger children – especially between the ages of six and nine – may be confused and need more reassurance that you aren't going anywhere. They may regress and act younger. Some teenagers may withdraw, act indifferent or become hostile and angry about the situation. Here are a few suggestions on how to handle them:

- Don't leave it until Mum or Dad's bags are packed and waiting in the hall. Give them time to adjust to things before one of you leaves.

- Reassure them that things will be okay and don't hold things back – be honest and they will respect you for it.

- Put your own needs first – don't feel you have to stay in an unhappy relationship for their sake. It will be better for everyone in the long run if you are happy.

- Don't drag them into arguments. Try to spare them the details. Equally, don't forget about them – keep them informed of what is happening and how you're coping. They learn from your behaviour.

- Don't bad-mouth your partner in front of the children. They will only feel confused and upset. Avoid putting them under pressure to take sides.

- Suggest that you go for family therapy if things aren't improving. This is a good way of making sure they aren't holding things in and becoming depressed. We'll talk about this more in Part 3.

A message for friends and family

Here is a message for your friends and family to read – so they can help you to get through this period.

Try to understand that this is a very difficult and painful time. Be non-judgemental and patient. Offer your practical and emotional support and be there if they need you in the short and long term. Don't feel that you have to take sides. The best thing is to remain neutral and supportive. Be sensitive – don't talk about their ex-partner too much but don't avoid the topic either. Accept that they need time and space and reassure them that you are there if they do want to talk. If you've been through a break-up yourself, no matter how long ago, what did you learn that you could share with them? Keep an eye on them and call from time to time, especially around difficult periods such as holidays when they might be feeling low. Someone who has taken the loss of a relationship very hard and is suffering from depression may become suicidal. Have you noticed any of the following behaviours?

- Do they appear withdrawn and flat?

- Are they not taking care of themselves?

- Are they tearful?

- Do they talk about ending it all?

- Are they not eating properly?

- Are they feeling worthless, a failure or suffering from low self-esteem?

It's normal to feel these emotions after a loss but if they persist, they will need help. If they choose to talk to you take what they say seriously. Be calm and encourage them to seek help from the Samaritans or another support organization. If they refuse to get help and you're worried then call yourself.

My closest friends knew that I was scared of him. My family were shocked because I'd never shown the strain I was under, as I wanted them to think I was okay. I hate failure and have learned a lot about being open with your life. My mum and dad were proud of me for leaving him and knew that it was better to do it now than in five years' time. They were terribly sad for me. I was the most dreamy and romantic of their four children and for me to have gone through all that was particularly difficult. My mother and brother called me every day to talk to me. I am particularly blessed. His family were gutted as I was the daughter they had always wanted. We have a good relationship now and his mum puts me in touch with my 'California self'. We get along well and are good friends although I'm not in contact with my ex.

Leanne

Your boss/colleagues

It's important that you tell your work colleagues for a number of reasons. You may have appointments and need time off. Your boss will be more agreeable if he or she knows why. Your boss will also understand why you're tired and non-productive and allow for this. Your human resources department may also be able to refer you for therapy at a reduced cost. You may be able to get time off as compassionate leave at your company's discretion. Your tax status may have changed so tell them about that too. Don't worry about office gossip – it's commonplace and people get bored and move on to other topics pretty quickly. If you work with your partner though, one of you may want to consider leaving and making a fresh start elsewhere.

6

You and your emotions

This chapter is about addressing your common worries and fears and dealing with recurrent emotions. Many people, for example, worry that they will be lonely and won't be able to cope on their own. Others experience terrible feelings of jealously that take over their whole lives. Some people find it very difficult to cope with feelings of anger and wonder if they'll ever be able to forgive and move on. If you're finding it difficult to cope do contact one of the organizations listed in Part 5.

Will you be lonely?

Yes, you will feel lonely from time to time. You've been used to having another person in your life and no matter how bad it was, sometimes that is preferable to being alone. However, give yourself a bit of time to get used to being on your own again and think about all the things you used to love to do. Are there new things you'd like to try? You have your freedom and independence and at first that can be a little scary. Soon, you will come to love it. Have a look at how you live – how social are you now and what can you do to increase this? Can you invite friends around for dinner more often, join new clubs or do some volunteer work? There are many groups and charities you can join – see your local library for details and Part 5 for listings.

Coping with feelings of jealousy

To begin with you might find the thought of your partner being with another person unbearable. So how can you stop feeling like this?

Jealousy is a destructive emotion. You might find yourself behaving irrationally – following your partner to work, calling him or her or trying to find out everything you can about the new person. You know it's destructive and it's making you unhappy but it's difficult to stop. It is fear that comes from low self-esteem. You might think that other people are more attractive and successful and you doubt your ability to hold a partner's interest. Ask yourself why you feel like this and it may also help to share your feelings with a counsellor. Read the section on self-esteem and concentrate on building yourself up.

Dealing with the 'low' days

Breaking up with a partner is never easy and you are bound to have low days. Losing someone you've loved since you were young or have been married to for many years can be even more difficult because you can't imagine your life without that person. If you've grown up together you will have been a huge influence on each other's lives. Take it one day at a time and get some support. Organizations such as Careline or Relate can be of great help (see Part 5, Chapter 15). Do remember that it's not a case of 'forgetting' someone – relationships shape us and make us who we are. Acknowledge the impact your partner had on your life and be thankful for what you shared and learned, however it ended.

If you feel low and depressed talk to your doctor, too, as he or she will be able to help. Depression can be treated and you will overcome it. Accept that you will need time to grieve and don't feel pushed into things by friends and family. Let them know that you are seeking treatment – and give them this book to read so they can understand how you're feeling.

Continuing a relationship with your ex

Sometimes partners will continue to sleep together after a break-up. It's one way of maintaining contact and because you're less familiar with each other sex can sometimes be better. There can be more emotion behind it or perhaps you're both a little afraid of letting go. You may be lonely and seeking comfort in the familiar. It could remind you of the beginning of your relationship when it was exciting and fresh. It may also give you a sense of control and power. Sometimes couples do this in the short term and then move on when they meet a new partner. It's not healthy because it makes it harder for you to heal and move on. Set a date for it to stop and stick to it. Try to have a clean break to give yourself closure. Try to deal with your feelings of loneliness and concentrate on filling your life with new people and events. Call a friend rather than your partner next time you feel tempted.

How can you stop yourself feeling so angry?

Anger is a normal process. It is a mixture of physical and emotional change in the body. It's important to release your anger otherwise it can impact upon your health and do you more harm than good in the long run. Try to work out what is making you feel this way. How can you deal with it constructively? What can you change and what do you need to accept about the situation? Know that you are in control and can deal with this. Next time you feel angry:

- Be assertive and don't shout

- Breathe slowly and deeply

- Do something physical or creative to release it – kick-boxing, running, screaming at the top of your voice in the countryside

- Write down how you're feeling

- Take three deep breaths. Inhale through your nose and breathe out slowly through your mouth

- Talk to your doctor if you feel it is becoming a problem.

Communicating with your ex

It's inevitable that you will have to meet your ex-partner to sort things out and it is often the case that you'll end up arguing. So how can you avoid this happening?

Lack of good communication is a common reason for relationship breakdown. Most couples have a certain style of communication and a way of dealing with conflict after the relationship breakdown. You might be upfront and face conflict head on or you might prefer to say nothing until your partner realizes something is wrong. You might be scared of arguments and go to great lengths to avoid them or you might try to find the best solution for both of you. Arguments can be productive – far better that you air your feelings than keep things bottled up. Here are some suggestions for improving communication:

- Choose a good time to talk.

- Agree an agenda for the chat and stick to it, but don't write it yourself and present it to your partner as an order.

- Talk about how you feel. Say 'I feel like this' rather than 'You make me feel...'

- Say what you think rather than what other people think.

- Sit opposite each other when you're talking and be aware of your body language and that of your partner.

- Breathe properly.

- Take 20 minutes each to talk about how you feel without the other interrupting so that you each get a chance to listen properly.

- Set a time limit for ending the conversation to avoid repeating yourselves.

Q. Some days I feel okay and others I just want the world to end. Am I always going to feel like this?

A. Accept that your emotions will be changeable for a little while. You've been through an ordeal and you need time to come to terms with things. Try to anticipate low days and things that might trigger them. Keep a diary and note anything down. Plan things to look forward to and make sure you are looking after yourself. Call a friend when you're feeling low or get out of the house and take a walk. Exercise will make you feel a whole lot better.

Feelings of regret

It's true that many people do regret ending a relationship. Four out of ten people regret getting divorced five years on and believe that they could have resolved things. However, you can only do what is best for you right now. Making the decision is often the hardest part and once you've done that you can take action. It sounds simple but writing a list of the pros and cons of having had your partner in your life can help you clarify things. Look back at the whole relationship not just the bits that were good. You will find peace in the knowledge that you did everything within your power to work things out.

Learning to forgive

Forgiveness isn't easy, especially if you feel that a partner has wronged you. You're still hurting and you may be feeling all sorts of emotions – anger, grief and wanting revenge. Over time this will ease and your feelings won't be so strong. Don't feel that you have to forgive instantly. Think of it as a process and give yourself some time to grieve and feel angry. It's about deciding to forgive yourself as well as your partner. You won't suddenly feel like it one day but over time you'll come to realize that not forgiving is holding you back from getting on with your life. Take it one day at a time and speak to a counsellor if you're really struggling with your feelings.

However, you may find that you can remain friends if enough time has passed and you've both come to terms with the situation. It's not likely to happen if you're still hurt and jealous at the thought of them having another partner, so give it a little time and make the effort to get your life back on track. Keep it civil if you've got things to sort out regarding property or if there are children to consider.

7

Practical lifelines

This chapter is all about you. It's about creating a new identity for yourself, working out what you want to do now and rebuilding your self-esteem. Self-esteem is how you view yourself. It's about the way you relate to yourself in terms of work, your friends, your achievements, your purpose in life, how you think other people view you, and your strengths and weaknesses. Low self-esteem is when you have a poor view of yourself in relation to those things and it's often why we choose to stay in unhealthy relationships. After a break-up your confidence may dip and you might be plagued by doubts such as: Will I meet someone else? or Why does everything I touch go wrong?

Here's a quick quiz to help you evaluate your self-esteem. Tick any boxes that you feel apply.

❏ Do you avoid social situations or people you know?
❏ Are you feeling anxious?
❏ Do you have issues with food – under-/over-eating?
❏ Do you feel unable to accept compliments?
❏ Do you focus on the negative?
❏ Are you neglecting yourself?
❏ Do you worry about what other people think?
❏ Do you feel reluctant to take on challenges?
❏ Do you feel that you don't expect much from life?

How did you do? If a few of the statements ring true then you need to tackle your feelings.

Here are some ways you can improve your self-esteem:

- Make a list of your positive qualities – physical and personality. What have friends said they like about you? Do you make people laugh? Do you have great dress sense? Are you a good listener?

- Create a photo wall of new places you'd like to visit when you can afford it or activities you've done recently and new people you've met. It will inspire you to do more and to keep working towards your goals.

- Keep up the exercise and relaxation.

- Make a list of things you'd like to change about your appearance and book one appointment a month. If money is an issue you can contact your local Adult Education college to find out about student clinics and training academies, which will be a lot cheaper.

- What other professional skills would you like to have? Can you study part-time or from home?

- Make a list of things you've always wanted to do – be it horse riding, sailing, travelling or other interests. You might be able to try things for free if you're interested in joining a club so it's worth calling up to find out. New activities will absorb you and it will help you to focus on other people rather than yourself. Contact the National Council for the Divorced and Separated (NCDS) – 0704 147 8120 – to find out what's going on in your area. Your local library will also have listings of activities.

It's important to feel well both physically and mentally. Draw a big circle on a piece of paper and divide it up into the following areas:

- Appearance

- Home life

- Career

- Health and wellbeing

- Relationships

- Family

- Money

- Spirituality.

How balanced do you feel in each area? What needs attention? Write down how you feel about yourself right now in each section and the things you'd like to change. If you lack close friends make an effort to get out more. Join some clubs, talk to people on a day-to-day basis. Be open and friendly. We don't always realize which areas need attention so this exercise is a helpful way of doing a quick overview.

Your appearance

How you look can have a huge impact on your mood and wellbeing. It's fairly easy to make some changes and it doesn't have to be radical although you might well feel like chopping off all your hair to make a statement! Book a hair appointment and be open to suggestions on new styles and colours. Some of the top salons have training academies so it won't cost you much. It's probably best not to go for anything too dramatic in the first few weeks as you might regret it! Make an appointment to see an image consultant – fees are flexible if you explain your circumstances – or ask a friend who has a flair for clothes to come shopping with you. Some department stores have a free personal shopping service and there's no pressure to buy. You can relax and try out new styles while someone else does the legwork for you.

If you're keen to lose a bit of weight then make a few changes. There are plenty of good books on healthy eating and that, combined with regular exercise, will help you to stay on top of things and look good. Find an exercise buddy if you're not feeling motivated to do it on your own. See Part 5, Chapter 16 for some useful websites.

Your home

Depending on the circumstances of the split you may be living in the same home or you may be living elsewhere temporarily. Whatever the situation try to make the best of it. Have your personal things around you and surround yourself with colourful, beautiful things that lift your spirits. A pretty print or a vase of fresh flowers can transform a room. Or try the photo wall we were talking about earlier. You might want to move to make a fresh start but if that's not possible right now think about redecorating so that you aren't reminded of your ex and can reclaim the space as your own. Create a boudoir that makes you feel sensual and feminine – a place that you can retreat to for time out. Keep a book that inspires you by your bed so you can read it at the beginning and end of each day. Your local library will have plenty of books to get you started.

Your career

Does your job fulfil you? Is there something else you've always wanted to do? Do you have enough money to retrain full-time or could you study part-time while you're working? Focusing on your career will help you through the difficult times and you'll feel like you are achieving something. Sometimes we hold ourselves back when we're in a relationship, so now is the time to get things moving again. There are several good books that can help you work out your personality type and the work that might suit you. Similarly, if you want to start a new business but you're not sure where to start, contact your local Business Link for ideas. Some employment agencies offer flexi-working and schemes, for example LearnDirect offers training and confidence boosting if you've been out of the workplace for a while. Contact your local library for details.

Your action plan:

- What is your current work situation? Does it fulfil your needs? What skills would you like to develop?

- What would be your dream job if money was not an issue? What steps would you need to take to get there?

- What are your good points? Ask a friend for feedback. If you've been at home bringing up the children, think about the skills you have acquired doing this: organization, time management, multi-tasking, and many more!

- Take small steps – apply for jobs that you can do now and consider training for the work you'd like to do in your spare time. If it's something you feel passionate about, finding the energy won't be a problem.

- Think about doing voluntary work in an area of interest – it will lead to new contacts and opportunities.

Your physical health

In times of stress it's very important to pay attention to your health. If you're ill it can be very hard to deal with things. Try to keep balanced and make time in your day for at least half an hour's exercise. Being fit will help you cope with mental stress.

- Watch your diet – don't overeat or drink for comfort.

- Walk around your local area and get to know it on foot.

- Check out your local gym for off-peak membership.

- Consider getting a dog if you have the time and money to look after one. You'll be motivated to walk it and it's a good way of meeting other people.

- Keep an eye on your alcohol consumption.

- Consider getting an allotment from the council. It's not only a great form of exercise, but you're growing your own veg and it's very sociable. A plot costs as little as £8 per year.

• Redecorate your house – it's a physical and mental workout and will help you to reclaim the space.

What you eat is very important in maintaining your physical and mental wellbeing. Make time at the weekends for cooking so you can freeze food and have healthy meals to eat during the week. Here are some foody tips to help you deal with stress:

• Eat two to three portions of oily fish a week (salmon or mackerel) as fish contains omega oils which are vital for mental energy. If you don't like fish or are a vegetarian or vegan, omega 3 supplements are available.

• Keep a little good quality dark chocolate in the fridge (at least 70 per cent cocoa) as it's good for your heart and will lift your mood.

• Cut down on coffee and fizzy drinks as they will make you feel jittery.

• Additives in some pre-prepared meals and fast foods can make you feel more stressed.

• Opt for some complex carbohydrates to help you keep going for longer – wholegrains and wholewheat pasta, rice and bread.

- Include protein for strength, for example, meat, fish, eggs, dairy and soya.

- Drink six to eight glasses of water a day. It's good for your skin, digestion and concentration.

- Avoid too much alcohol – it's a depressant.

Relaxation exercises

It's important that you take time out to relax to help your body recover from stress. Most of us run from one thing to another and collapse in a heap at the end of the day. Making a few small changes to your day will go a long way to helping you feel more in control. Be purposeful – join a gym, start your day with a morning walk or some tai'chi. Listen to uplifting music when you're travelling home.

Deep breathing exercises

These will help to calm a racing mind. When you're stressed for long periods it weakens your immune system and your body retaliates by giving up and becoming ill. You might find yourself unable to concentrate, feeling moody and tearful, depressed or unable to sleep.

Put your hands on your chest and stomach and take a few deep breaths to see where you're breathing. Breathe deeply until you can feel your stomach expand rather than your chest. This sends more oxygen to your brain. It might feel a little odd at first because you're used to breathing shallowly, so persevere.

- Do a few stretches to relax your body. Sit quietly on your own. Take a few deep breaths and close your eyes.

- Tense and relax each of your muscles. Don't worry if you get distracted by your thoughts – imagine them floating away.

- Visualize a place that you feel really happy in.

- Stay in this position for at least 15 minutes.

Here are some ideas to try out when you are feeling stressed:

- Write down what is worrying you before you go to bed each night. You can't do anything about it until tomorrow so you might as well get a night's rest.

- Plan days in your diary to relax and do nothing.

- Keep any 'to do' lists short and aim to tackle a couple of items a day.

- Carry some lavender essential oil around with you and put a few drops on a tissue when you feel stressed.

- Have a check up with your doctor. If you feel continually anxious and on edge there may be something physically wrong that can be resolved.

- Be mindful and practise a little meditation each day. This can be as simple as noticing the food you're eating, taking in your surroundings and listening properly. Sit for five minutes a day on your own, do some deep breathing and notice how your thoughts come and go.

- Take each day as it comes and live in the moment. Be purposeful about your actions.

Your sexuality

Everyone is different with regard to their sexuality so do what is right for you. You might have no interest in sex at all or you may feel like having a casual relationship. Fulfil your own needs without hurting anyone or getting hurt yourself.

Make an effort to keep in touch with your sexuality. You can do this in many ways, for example, by reading erotica, looking at art, thinking about how you choose to express yourself physically and through self-touch. Exercise will help hugely because it lifts your mood and helps you to view your body more positively. Make an effort with conversation when you meet people and don't be afraid to flirt a little. Wear fabrics you feel good in and invest in some new lingerie. Think about smells and perfume, how your bedroom is furnished, lighting in your home and how that affects your mood. Give yourself a massage after a bath using nice body creams and book an aromatherapy massage once a month if you can afford it. You're not being indulgent – touch therapy is essential for wellbeing particularly after a break-up because you've lost that physical connection.

Your mental health

Relationship breakdown is one of the most stressful things you will face in life. It is easy to tackle the physical things but it's not always so easy to figure out what is going on in your head. It's a good idea to speak to a counsellor or therapist to help you gain some perspective on the situation and to come to terms with it if you're struggling to deal with your feelings. There is only so much you can do on your own.

Try to broaden your social circle. You can do this by taking up new hobbies and interests. Consider some solo travel or join a travel site on the internet that fixes you up with other people who are looking for a travel companion. Be open to new things, for example, your library noticeboard will have details of clubs you can join. If you're on your own with the children the charity Gingerbread organizes social events and holidays for single parents.

Here's an overview of the different types of therapy and how they can help you:

Counselling and psychotherapy

You can talk about your feelings in a private and confidential setting with a counsellor. It can help you to see things more clearly and from a different perspective and is non-judgemental. Generally you will be offered around ten sessions at an hour a time. There isn't any real distinction between counselling and psychotherapy although it depends on the context in which it's being offered. You can contact your GP or Careline for free/low cost therapy services. You can also contact the British Assocation for Counselling and Psychotherapy (BACP) to find a therapist (see Part 5, Chapter 15), the average fee will be around £35 per hour.

Cognitive behavioural therapy

A talking therapy that looks at how our thinking processes influence our actions and how we feel. It can be used to treat depression, anxiety and distorted thinking and can help you to replace negative thinking patterns with more positive ones.

Complementary therapy

This can help alleviate stress, anxiety and depression. The aim of each therapy is to be holistic – to look at the whole person rather than individual symptoms and to help your body heal itself. Here are some examples of complementary therapy:

- **Herbal medicine** – this involves using plant extracts to treat illness. St John's Wort may be helpful in treating depression, although you should always speak to your doctor first before taking any herbal medicines. You can find a qualified herbalist through the National Institute of Medical Herbalists.

- **Acupuncture** – this is a form of Chinese medicine and in the East is used as a preventative measure to help the body stay healthy. It involves using fine needles to stimulate various energy (chi) points throughout the body. It can help with depression, anxiety, headaches, muscular pains and addiction.

- **Touch therapy** – massage is highly beneficial for your health and wellbeing, particularly if you don't have daily contact with another person. Aromatherapy massage involves using essential oils with different properties. Some are relaxing, some balancing and others stimulating. They can enhance wellbeing and help you to move forward emotionally. Once you know what certain oils do you can buy them yourself and use them at home in the bath or a burner.

- **Visualization** – this is sometimes used in hypnotherapy as a way of helping you to deal with negative feelings and difficult scenarios. It involves using your imagination to heal yourself. You may be asked to picture yourself in a situation when you felt confident, happy and positive. Recreating those emotions triggers a part of the brain that will help you to relax.

- **Affirmations** – this can be very powerful. It involves writing down how you want to feel or how you want your life to be as though it already is, for example, 'I am a confident, outgoing person.' Writing these statements repeatedly and reading them often helps your brain to accept that they are reality.

- **Creative therapy** – if you find it hard to talk about your emotions and would rather express yourself physically then channelling your emotions into art, writing, dance or drama can be healing. Dance helps to ease depression as well as freeing you from rigid thoughts. Discovering you have a talent for something will boost your self-esteem and confidence and it's a great way to meet new people.

It could be helpful to see a life coach or a divorce coach to help you get back on track. A quick internet search will throw up dozens so use your common sense and go via an organization such as The International Coach Federation. Ask around to see if any friends can recommend anyone and contact previous coachees to see how they found it. Most coaches will offer a free trial session to see if you can work together. There needs to be a rapport between you and you should come away from each session feeling energized and motivated. Coaching aims to address the present and future, unlike therapy, which looks at the past to make sense of where you are now. It can help you to work on your goals and boost your confidence and self-esteem.

Workshops

Relate offers a course called 'Moving Forward: After a divorce or break-up', which takes place over a day or a few evening sessions to help you gain perspective on the end of your relationship. It can be very helpful in identifying relationship patterns and you will meet other people who are in the same situation as you. There are also divorce recovery workshops, which aim to do the same. See Part 5, Chapter 15 for further details.

Internet forums

These can be a very helpful way of gaining perspective on your situation and interacting with other people who have shared your experiences. It's free and you can ask questions and talk openly and honestly, even anonymously, if you wish.

Part 3: Longer-term Challenges and Future Hopes

In this part we're going to look at how things are for you further down the line – one year on. You will have come to terms with the situation and found your own ways of dealing with things. Time is a great healer and you've done a lot of work on yourself over the past few months. As the months go by you will be feeling more in control and you will find yourself thinking about your relationship less. There will still be good and bad days, of course, and you may find yourself overcome with emotion at certain times of the year – anniversaries, Christmas, birthdays, holidays – when you may find yourself going over old ground. There will be a turning point at which you start to think that you've wallowed in the past for long enough and want to get things moving again. We'll look at how you can rebuild your networks and start dating again and how you can ease yourself back in to it.

Getting through the first year after a break-up is an achievement. You'll be constantly reminded of the past and you may have to deal with difficult issues with your family and your ex-partner's family. So, congratulate yourself on getting this far. The best thing you can do is to really get to know yourself and what you want from life and to focus on building a life that *you* want and feel happy and comfortable in. Once you have reached this stage you will make new relationships and they will be healthy ones that will last.

Your needs will have changed now. Perhaps you were married with children and you don't want to do all that again. You want to meet new people, have fun and enjoy being sexual. Your children come first and anyone you meet has to recognize that. Maybe you would like company at the weekends because you're busy working and doing your own thing during the week, or you're thinking about travelling on your own for a while. Perhaps you've already met someone else but you're a little nervous about getting burned again. You want to protect yourself, retain a little independence and make sure that you're financially secure for the future. We will give you some tips later on in Chapter 11 about protecting yourself financially if you do decide to remarry or live with a new partner.

The aim of this part of the book is to help you to have a bit of fun, to expand your horizons a bit and to take you out of your comfort zone. We will help you build up your networks so that you feel confident and relaxed in social situations. Whatever your circumstances right now you're probably keen to make new friends and contacts for personal and professional reasons.

Finding out who you are is a life-long process and each day you are a different person with different needs. Often, when you're in a long-term relationship you don't stop to think about whether your needs are being met. There's a tendency to go along with things, to do things for your partner, and it's easy to lose sight of yourself in the process. Now you've had a bit of time to reflect on your life you will realize that being on your own is a positive state to be in. You know yourself a lot better, you feel stronger and you've had time to do the things that you've wanted to do. It is a healthy state of mind to be in – when you realize that you can provide for yourself, you have a lovely life on your own, and that having someone to share all of that with would be a bonus rather than a necessity.

8

Emotional lifelines

Sit on your own with a notepad and pen for a few minutes and reflect on your relationship. Write down how you felt immediately after the break-up – just one or two words to describe your feelings. On the next page do the same for one month later, six months and then one year later – how you're feeling now. When you've finished, tear the pages out and line them up so you can get a quick overview of how your feelings have changed. It won't necessarily be a progression but you will be able to see how your feelings have changed over time. Don't spend too long agonizing over it – just jot down what comes to mind when you think back. This will clarify how you have changed over the past year.

Here are a few of the emotions you may be experiencing now:

- Acceptance
- Freedom
- Confidence
- Feeling comfortable in your own skin
- Strength
- Self-awareness
- Feeling focused
- Feeling single-minded.

Coping with anniversaries

You have rebuilt your life and moved on, setting yourself new goals and taking each day as it comes. However, there will still be times during the year when you feel emotional and this can set you back a bit. Certain times of the year are loaded with memories and if you can anticipate them and prepare in advance it will be easier to cope when the time comes. Keeping yourself busy during these times will help.

Wedding anniversaries

The first year of an anniversary will be difficult if you were together for a long time and it might seem like the date is etched into your brain! Make a plan ahead of time and do something positive for yourself to mark your progress.

Avoid putting dates on the calendar if you can – or buy a new one. Eventually those significant dates will become less so as you fill your time with new interests and people. Buy yourself a little memento to celebrate a year on your own and the things you've achieved since then.

Divorce day

If you were married and your divorce has finally come through you will have mixed feelings. It's a huge day for you emotionally and loaded with significance. You may be feeling a range of emotions, for example, relief, freedom, sadness, nostalgia and happiness. Plan for it and do something uplifting. Have people around to support you and mark the day with something positive for yourself – be it a new haircut, outfit or something creative to do. Be kind to yourself.

Don't be too hard on yourself – accept that there will be little reminders and times when you feel sad at the loss or have the flash of a past memory. This won't last long and when you've been through it once it gets easier. Important dates will gradually lose their significance and be replaced by other things. Every time you feel low allow yourself to feel that way for ten minutes and then get up and do something else.

Celebrations and holidays

Birthdays

On your birthday pamper yourself and do something different. Take a day trip with friends or try a new activity.

On your ex-partner's birthday keep yourself busy so you're not dwelling on it too much and thinking about the celebrations. Make plans for the evening.

As far as your children's birthdays are concerned, prepare for the day in advance so that it runs as smoothly as possible. Make it exciting for them and try to agree on who does what this year. Don't view it as a competition or think that you need to spend lots of money to prove your love. It's a day for the children to remember and they will value the opportunity to spend time with you regardless of what you do. Plan presents in advance so that you and your ex-partner don't buy the same things.

Christmas

Advance planning is key at Christmas. If you're on your own you may be thinking about last Christmas and what you were all doing, and feeling sad because you and your partner are no longer doing things together with the children, if you have them. Many people find Christmas a very difficult time of year because expectations are so high and you feel like you should be having a jolly time. In reality it can be very lonely. Remember that it's only two days of the year – one weekend, that's all. If you're on your own this year, can you spend it with friends or go away and do something completely different? It will be trickier if children are involved so plan things ahead of time. Arrange who will have the children on which day and discuss presents in advance.

Christmas is a time for the children and it will be memorable if you are happy and relaxed so keep things low key with lots of good cooking, comedy TV and regular and comforting routines. It's not about how much you spend; the time you have together and what you talk about is so much more important. Try to make it as special and relaxed a time as possible. Make some New Year resolutions to get things off to a positive start.

You may find it difficult especially if everyone is off out celebrating and you're not really in the mood. Try to generate a sense of excitement and renewal for the New Year and all the positive things to come.

Celebrations

Celebrations such as weddings or engagement parties can be tough, especially if you were engaged or married. It's wonderful to be able to help people celebrate their special day but being surrounded by loving couples and families with children may make you feel completely alone. Plus they may be nosy and want to know what's happened. You might find it helpful to take a friend with you. You could turn up for the service just before it starts and leave straight after or go to the meal (limit your drinking!) and leave once all the formal speeches are done. Things like this do get easier over time so know your limits and be kind to yourself.

Holidays

Holidays and bank holidays can be a very stressful time if you have children and it's often difficult to make arrangements so try to do so as early as possible. Again, try not to be competitive and feel that you and your ex-partner need to outdo each other in terms of money and excitement factor. Keep things simple – short distance holidays may work better than long haul if the children are young. Long car journeys can be difficult. If you don't have children plan a special trip for yourself or go with a friend. Try something you've never done before, perhaps an adventure or creativity break. Avoid revisiting places that you went to with your ex. There were probably things you would have liked to have done when you were together but didn't because your partner didn't fancy it. Do them now. Holidays can be healing if you choose wisely.

Your survival kit – the first year

Here are some suggestions to help you move on:

- Put all keepsakes and mementos in a box in the attic or get rid of them so they aren't a daily reminder. Replace them with new photos of places you're planning to visit and gifts from new friends.

- Buy a new calendar and diary and don't mark old dates.

- Plan activities throughout the year so you have things to look forward to – especially at Christmas or on birthdays.

- Start some creative endeavours.

- Look for new work that fulfils and absorbs you.

- Review your exercise and diet and how you feel physically.

- Keep a list of your goals and achievements.

- Review your finances and make sure you are happy with the settlement and have finalized things with your ex-partner.

- Create a new bedroom for yourself that reflects who you are.

- Keep friendships going and aim to find new ones.

9

Rebuilding
relationships

This chapter focuses on how your relationships are now that some time has passed. Are you happy with current arrangements? Are you and your ex-partner still in contact and is it working out? Would you like to change things in some way? If you're not in contact or if family relations are strained we'll look at ways you can improve this.

Have you done all you can to repair family relations since the split? There is only so much you can do so accept that and don't expect things to be perfect or as they were before. You can't wave a magic wand, rewrite history or control people's behaviour. Families can be very difficult to deal with at times and emotions can be buried and run deep. Give it time and make sure that you have supportive friends around you to help you deal with any difficult times.

Q: What is family therapy?

A: It involves a therapist spending time with your family over a set period of time to see how you interact and to suggest ways to deal with common problems. It can help you to see that what is perceived as one person's issue can actually stem from the whole family dynamic and so to address it you all need to change the way you think and behave. It can be useful support if you are struggling with the children's behaviour, if things aren't getting better over time and you feel too exhausted to deal with it all. Your doctor will be able to refer you to a therapist locally. There is more information in Part 5.

Your children

Perhaps your relationship with the children is okay now – they have come around, accept the new situation and see their mother or father regularly. They may be urging you to get on with your life in the same way and to stop spending so much time on your own. On the other hand, if the split was difficult and prolonged they may feel torn between the two of you. They may feel as if they are to blame in some way and as a result their behaviour changes. There may be issues at school or they may be spending time with people you don't approve of. If they are withdrawn and refusing to talk to you or let you into their lives it can be very hard to deal with, but try to accept it as a phase that they will grow out of. In a worst-case scenario, they may be hostile and violent towards you or run away from home and if this is the case then you need to get help. You could consider having family therapy for a while.

All you can do is provide a loving home and an established routine so that they know there is room to talk if they want to. Be upfront and honest about the relationship and why it ended and try not to be bitter about it. Your happiness is important, too, because it sets the tone for your children who are watching you to see how you are coping. You are a role model for them in terms of how you handle things and they will learn from your behaviour. They will have spoken to friends about the break-up – many of their friends will have been through it and so they will understand more than you think or perhaps give them credit for.

Relations may be strained if you've uprooted to find a new home and the children have had to start afresh at a new school and have had to find new friends. There may be less money than before and a change in lifestyle to deal with which, in turn, brings its own resentments. Try to keep up the routines, continue to talk, and treat it as a big adventure for all of you. Get out and do things in your new area and make an effort to meet people. Explain that money is tight and you will need to do things differently for a while. In many ways the less money you have the more creative you will have to be with your time. This can be more enriching for the children. Spend your time together doing simple things such as cooking a nice meal or going for long walks instead of buying expensive gifts to compensate for your lack of time or feelings of guilt.

Show them that, deep down, nothing has

changed. You and your partner may not be together but you both love the children equally and are making the best of the situation. Give it time and don't expect immediate acceptance of the situation. Think about your old family roles – who did what and who was responsible for what? How have things changed and what do you need to re-establish? If you are the decision maker now, show some authority and stick to your decisions so that they acknowledge that. Don't let them walk all over you because you feel guilty.

All of this is much harder to deal with if you are a single parent so if you are feeling overwhelmed then talk to a friend, counsellor or an organization such as Gingerbread or the National Council for the Divorced and Separated (NCDS), which offers support, friendship and social functions (see Part 5, Chapter 15 for details).

Your families

Hopefully things will have settled down since the early days and both your families will be more accepting and understanding of the situation. They can see that it's for the best and that you are both happier now. It may be difficult if you were close to your ex-partner's family because inevitably, you won't be seeing them so much now. But as we said before there's no reason why you need to cut contact. Once you've both had time to readjust and are over the break-up then you can start to repair and rebuild things with the family. Take it slowly as you will all need to re-establish your roles and what happens now. In a worst-case scenario they may still blame you or feel hostile and refuse to see you. All you can do is explain your side of things and accept how they feel for now. It will change over time and it will help you to talk to someone else about how you're feeling. Try to keep the lines of communication open and concentrate on getting on with your own life in the meantime. Try to avoid getting involved in family dramas or arguments about the relationship – you and your ex know the details and what everyone else thinks is unimportant.

Your ex-partner

You will both be moving on with your lives at your own pace. In an ideal world you would stay in touch and be amicable. However, you may not want that, especially if the split was painful for you, and it might be easier not to be in touch and to sever all ties. You or your partner may have moved away to start afresh, which will make things easier. If you have children then it's likely that you will still be very much a part of each other's lives in terms of visits and practical and financial arrangements so try to keep things amicable with minimal disruption for the children. They will learn from your behaviour so how you handle the split is important.

My husband and I met when we were 17 so you could say we were childhood sweethearts. Things were good for some time but I gradually realized that we had grown apart and we no longer wanted the same things in life. We moved from London to Buckinghamshire and I think he just wanted to settle down and enjoy the country life. But I felt that my life – and my work – was in London and I knew I wouldn't be happy there. Luckily there were no children to think about, as that would have made things more difficult.

In the end the split was amicable and we're still good friends and see each other around once a month. I think you need to make a decision to be kind to one another. There's no reason why a break-up has to be awful. Show respect for each other and for what you had and don't destroy your partner's self-esteem.

Both of us dated after a while but we weren't looking for anything serious. I just wanted to prove to myself that I was out there being proactive. I ran a mile from men who were looking for any

*kind of commitment, as I just wasn't
ready. In the end I met a gorgeous
younger man who worked wonders on
my self-esteem. He said 'tell me what
you want and I'll do anything.' That
gave me a boost and it was exactly what
I needed at the time. It helped me to
regain my confidence around men.*

*I realize now that I have a very nice
life. I enjoy my work. I'm successful and
I don't need a partner for the sake of it.
I value myself, and my life and I've
learned how to enjoy having a lover.*

Marianne

10

What do you want now?

Before you're ready to have a new relationship it's important to have a period of introspection to get to know who you really are, to understand yourself and what you're looking for in a potential partner and how your relationships have been so far. You need to feel relaxed and happy in your own company before you enter into a new relationship. It will help to consider your parents' relationship and how it has shaped your own views and attitudes.

Getting to know the real you

Earlier on in Chapter 5 we asked you to write about how you were feeling immediately after the break-up. Read it again to remind yourself of how you were feeling and ask yourself the following questions:

- What do you want from a relationship now?

- What else do you want from life? What do you want to achieve?

- What attracted you to your previous partner – did he or she give you strength in a certain area?

- What have you learned from your previous relationships?

- Do you have a 'type' or certain characteristics you look for in a partner and where do you think these come from?

- How was your life when you met your partner? Were you happy and balanced or feeling needy and desperate? Had you recently come out of a previous relationship when you met?

- What was your parents' relationship like? How was the atmosphere at home when you were growing up? Did they show affection and warmth towards each other? Did they love each other?

- How long have you spent on your own after a relationship has ended thinking about things?

- How does being alone make you feel?

- How do you talk about previous partners? Is it with fondness or are you still bitter and angry? Do you blame other people for your situation and how you feel?

- Why didn't it work out? What was your part in that? Was it lack of time, communication or misguided expectations? Was there a lack of commitment or trust?

- Think about the qualities your partner had that annoyed you – insecurity or neediness, for example. We often unconsciously choose people who have similar qualities to ourselves because we feel comfortable with them. If your partner has certain qualities that annoy you, consider how developed these characteristics are in yourself. What can you do to change? If you don't address this now you will attract someone else who has these traits.

- What are your expectations now? Are you looking for another serious relationship or a casual fling?

- How are you meeting new people right now? How comfortable do you feel with the idea of socializing or dating again? Have you tried it already and how did it make you feel?

- What is your work/life balance like now? What do you need to change to put you in a better situation socially or to meet someone new?

- How is your health and fitness? Are you eating properly and taking care of yourself? Are you happy with the way you look?

- What assumptions do you have about yourself that you need to change? We all have that little voice that sits on our shoulder and pipes up every now and then – 'I'll be happy when I'm thin' or 'I need a partner to be happy' or 'I'm rubbish at relationships, they never work out.' If you do catch yourself having these thoughts be aware of them and let them go. They are transient and will often pop up when you're feeling low. Meditation will help, as will keeping a diary. Both help you to gain perspective and distance on your thoughts.

Asking yourself these questions will make you more aware of how things are and what you want *now*. They will help you to examine your behaviour and the past, to see why you've created the life and relationships you have had. They will help you to move forward and create a life you want. Talk things through with a good friend or a counsellor if you need help in a certain area or are struggling to understand your feelings. Once you've reached a state of emotional health then you'll be able to attract positive relationships into your life that aren't based on need. Things will be easier for you the next time around because you have so much more experience and self-awareness and you know what you want and don't want from life and relationships.

Four things you can do for yourself this week:

- Pursue an interest or hobby that you didn't do when you were with your partner because it took up too much of your time.

- Visit a place you've never been to before.

- Call a friend you've not spoken to in a while.

- Eat something that you've never tried before.

What are rebound relationships?

Many of us get involved in unsuitable or transitory relationships after a break-up. A casual fling is okay if you accept it for what it is and it can be the ego boost you need. But often we get involved with people too quickly because we feel sad, desperate or lonely. You might do it out of revenge or guilt or simply to prove to yourself or your ex-partner that you are attractive and desirable and that you have moved on. See a rebound relationship for what it is – temporary. It is about getting you back out there, feeling confident and being physical with another person again. You may feel relieved initially not to be single again but then you may grow dissatisfied and go your separate ways. This cycle can keep repeating itself if you don't address it. Do it too often and it can affect your confidence and self-esteem. You use the person as a prop to stop you feeling the pain from a previous relationship. This can be hurtful to the person you're involved with, as they may be wanting more from you and the relationship.

Ask yourself:

- How do you really feel about this person? Are you interested in them or are they a distraction from other things? Is it just about sex for you?

- How soon did you get involved with them after your previous relationship ended? Rebound relationships often grow intense very quickly – you may not be thinking straight or making balanced decisions.

- Have you changed the way you normally act to attract a person? Are you not being yourself?

- What characteristics does your new partner have? Are they very different from your ex-partner? Have you chosen someone that you feel you can manipulate?

- Do you still dwell on your previous relationship and think about your ex-partner a lot?

If you're not sure how you feel or whether this is a rebound relationship then try to take things slowly and see what develops. Don't make any rash decisions on your future together.

The dating game

If you've been on your own for a while and have started to think about dating again then you may find this section helpful. If you are not ready for a new relationship right now, concentrate on exploring and developing your own interests and setting yourself some goals to achieve. You can come back to this section later on if and when you feel ready. Be aware that the first relationship you have after a significant break-up is likely to be emotional, as it will bring things up for you again. Take it slowly and meet people on your terms. Be happy in your own company first.

Attracting a partner

By thinking about the questions in the last section you've already made progress. Quite often we fall into relationships without really thinking about what we want and need from a partner. Then we get disappointed when they don't work out. You can prevent this from happening by analysing things and thinking about what you really want and need from people. It may sound a bit harsh or businesslike but it's worth giving your personal life the same attention and detail that you would give to your job. Why shouldn't you plan it out? It's not unromantic. You set goals in most areas of your life and have a clear idea of the work, type of house or car that you want so it makes sense to apply that determination and focus to attracting the type of person you want to share your life with. Why should you settle for less that you deserve?

Attraction exercise

Visualize your ideal partner. Write down their qualities and how your life is together. Describe it in detail. How do you feel when you're around this person? What qualities do you want and not want? What are your needs and what makes you feel special and loved? Are there areas that you are willing to compromise on? For example, you'd rather have someone who likes the outdoors but it's not the be all and end all. Be specific about what is very important to you and cannot be compromised. Think about your past relationships and what didn't work for you. It might feel a bit odd doing this exercise because it's not something you would normally do. It will build a sense of excitement and anticipation because you are focusing on your goals and what you want – and you will be drawing this person into your life.

A numbers game

It is often said that you need to kiss a lot of frogs to meet a prince and there is some truth in that. Sometimes we settle and stop looking for a soul mate because our expectations or self-esteem are low and we don't believe we can attract any better. You might have had a number of poor relationships and have come to think that that is how life is. But since then you've done lots of work on building up your self-esteem and the type of person you attract will reflect that. You might not have met the right person because you haven't dated enough to know what it is you do and don't want from a relationship. You need to compare and date different types of people to see which qualities do and don't work for you. Don't be so specific that you rule people out before getting to know them. Sometimes we can be afraid of dating and the expectations around it and this holds us back. We don't approach people because we're afraid of rejection.

What are your options?

There are many ways to meet new people – the internet being increasingly popular. There are also singles' events, holidays, friends and work, dating agencies, personal ads, and day-to-day life, hobbies and interests and local business networks. Whatever your chosen method – and we'll have a look at a few of those in a minute – try to approach it as a fun game, with the aim of meeting as many new people as possible.

Challenge your preconceptions and go out with people whom you wouldn't normally consider meeting. The aim is to build up your networks and social life, as this will benefit you in many areas of life – professionally as well as personally. Set a time limit on it if you wish and have a breather so you can review the people you've met, what you're looking for now and what conclusions you've made. You may surprise yourself. As we said before, it's likely that your needs will have changed – you may not be looking for a full-time relationship anymore. You may be busy with your work or children and want something that fits in with your new lifestyle. Other areas of your life may take prominence and you won't have as much time, so you may want to take things slowly.

Start locally. What is the area like where you live? Is it fairly metropolitan or do you live in the country? That will make a difference, although it can sometimes be far easier to meet people in the country as people tend to have more time to spare! Check your library noticeboard and local paper for ads for classes and courses. Book groups, comedy clubs and exercise classes are usually good ways to meet people and will be less pressured because the focus is on something else. People are also more likely to go more than once. College or night classes are also worth doing – you'll be expanding your knowledge and doing something you're interested in so you are more likely to have something in common with other people on the course.

Task for this week

Arrange to meet some new people through your friends. Don't take it too seriously – the aim is to get out and have fun and expand your networks a bit.

Think about the things you do daily and try to make them more social – eat out from time to time, go for coffee, chat to people in the shops, on the bus or at the gym. Notice who is buying meals for one in the supermarket! Make an effort to talk to at least three new people every day. It doesn't matter how casual the conversation is – everyone has networks so you never know who you might be introduced to. Keep yourself busy and up to date with the news so that you have things to talk about when you do get chatting.

If there's nothing much going on locally then consider starting something up yourself. A book group if you like reading, a walking group, cooking class – whatever interests you. If it's a regular event people will get to know about it and it's a great way of getting to know people in your area, especially if you've recently moved there. Setting a regular time aside for networking will benefit you professionally as well as personally and it will get you known in your area. It will also boost your confidence and you may find you enjoy it. Bringing people together can be rewarding. If your home is unsuitable or too small, consider hiring a community hall or meeting in a corner of the local pub. No one will mind as long as the group buys a few drinks!

Internet dating

Around 8 million people in the UK use the internet for dating and it's an increasingly popular way to meet a partner. It's quick, accessible and you'll meet a large number of people who are also looking for a partner. You can do it from home, in your pyjamas, whenever it suits you, so it's great if you have children and don't have the time or money to go out. It can add a little fun and flirtation to your daily life and also builds confidence. You can send a 'wink' to someone you like the look of!

Sometimes it's easier to be more relaxed and honest when you are behind the anonymity of a screen. On the flipside, people do exploit this sometimes. You need to be cautious and keep your wits about you. People do lie on the internet and you might find out the person you've been happily chatting to intimately is married with children.

People are often looking for casual sex or extra marital encounters so it's best to be aware of this. Keep your expectations realistic and don't let yourself get hurt emotionally by getting involved with someone too soon. You don't have to meet people – you can limit it to email chat if you wish, or friendship rather than a relationship.

Here are some tips for successful dating on the internet:

- Be creative with your profile so that people are curious and want to meet you.

- People are seven times more likely to look at your profile if you have a photo on the site. Choose a good quality one that shows you at your best and says something about who you are.

- Be honest about what you want – be it a short- or longer-term relationship.

- Choose your sites carefully and consider paying for a professional one. You know that the people on it will also be serious about finding a partner.

- If you have certain hobbies that take up a lot of your time look for niche sites aimed at those hobbies so you'll be meeting someone with the same interests as you.

- Aim to meet people sooner rather than later. Chat on the phone if distance is involved and use a web cam.

- Some sites offer a free trial to prospective

members so this is a good way to test the water if you're not sure.

If you're slightly nervous about internet dating then recruit a single friend to do it with you. You can compare notes and it will take the pressure off somewhat so you don't take it too seriously. You'll enjoy the whole experience a lot more if you have someone you can share it with.

Online networking sites like Ecademy, MySpace or Facebook are another good way of expanding your contacts because you can meet friends of friends. You can join all types of groups and events for business or personal networking and you'll meet a wide range of people from all over the world.

Caution

As with any form of dating be careful and safe when you meet people. Give a friend information about your date and where/when you are meeting. Always arrange to meet in a public place and don't be afraid to cut things short if you aren't feeling comfortable.

Singles' events

Speed-dating

Here, you have a couple of minutes to chat to several men or women so the advantages are that you'll meet a high number of people in one evening. Events are usually held in a nice bar or restaurant. It can be quite tiring because you have to make conversation with lots of people as well as try to remember the names of people you'd like to talk to again. However, once you get into the flow of things it can be great fun. There's no pressure to make an instant decision about someone because you can note down someone's name or number and contact them via the website or ask the host to put you in touch later on.

Here are some tips for successful speed-dating:

- Make an effort with your clothing – it's all about first impressions but make sure you wear something you feel comfortable in.

- Gen up on the latest news and current affairs for easy conversation starters.

- Know a little bit about the venue.

- Think of some questions to ask people beforehand.

- Go with some friends to make the evening more enjoyable.

- Don't take it too seriously and aim to have fun.

Other singles' events include larger gatherings with extras, such as workshops and talks to smaller dinner parties where you'll meet around 10 to 15 people. These can be good value for money because you'll meet a lot of people in one evening and have a nice dinner inclusive in the price. It can also take the pressure off a bit, as it's not a one-to-one encounter.

Singles' holidays

This might seem quite daunting at first, especially if you've never been on holiday on your own before. However, the number of single people is on the increase and travel companies have recognized this. These days you'll find a good range of fun holidays that won't cost you the earth if travelling alone. It can be a lot more intimate because it's a shared experience and you will get to know people over a period of time. You're quite likely to make some good friends and you'll enjoy the trip regardless because you're being stimulated by new things. It can be a good way to start rebuilding networks and to boost your confidence if you enjoy travelling but don't want to go alone. You can take part in a range of activities including adventure holidays, creativity breaks or cooking classes. If it's a hobby that interests you then you'll be meeting other people with the same interests and developing your skills at the same time. Trips that are physically demanding such as a walking or mountain trek will put you in a better frame of mind, push you out of your comfort zone and increase your confidence. They can help to heal any emotional blocks that you've been holding on to since the break-up. If money is an issue it's always worth asking if you can pay in instalments. Ask if you can speak to one of their previous participants to find out how it was.

Dating agencies

There are a lot of agencies out there catering for different clientele. They can be useful if you're short on time and money isn't an issue. You get the benefit of a personal touch and things are organized for you so there's very little effort required on your part to spend time looking for a partner. You may get a set number of dates a year and will usually meet in nice venues. It can feel safer as you know that each person has been vetted by the agency. Another advantage is that it can help to have an outside perspective – you may be surprised to find that you hit it off with someone you would never have chosen for yourself. The matchmaker has a hunch that you might get on, even though on paper you seem to be opposites and that's always a nice surprise.

The downside is the cost and the fact that you don't know how much attention to detail goes into the matching process. If you are considering using an agency go for one that is vetted by the Association of British Introduction Agencies (ABIA).

Classified ads

This is still quite a popular way of meeting people because it's cheap and there's something a little old-fashioned and charming about browsing the paper over breakfast to find a date. You write a brief description of what you're looking for and people contact you, usually by leaving a message on a voicemail box, which can be a nice way of building up a friendship or relationship. Unlike internet personals there are no photos to look at so initially you are making a decision based on words and a telephone conversation. Ads also tend to be quite short and therefore not particularly targeted. To be successful using this method it's best to stick to conventional wording in your ad, for example, words such as 'genuine', 'caring' or 'humorous' have been proven to be popular.

As with internet dating use your common sense and be cautious when meeting people for the first time.

Networking tips

Here are a few things to consider when you're meeting new people:

- Make an effort with your appearance. Pay attention to detail – your hands and nails. Little things send a message to someone about how you value and take care of yourself. Make the effort to look good at all times not just on special occasions – you never know who you might bump into at the supermarket. Looking good will boost your self-esteem and confidence and you will be more likely to talk to other people. When you feel positive other people pick up on that so you will be more approachable. Plus, if you're wearing something unusual people will ask you about it – always a good conversation starter. You don't have to spend a lot of money – it's more about your individual style and what your clothes and accessories say about you as a person.

- Start trying to meet people locally. Look for advertised groups or start up your own networking evening.

- If you're using the internet to date, try to meet up with people sooner rather than later. Prolonged chat online can build up a sense of expectation and fantasy around a person, which doesn't necessarily translate when you meet them in the flesh, and you might be setting yourself up for disappointment. If distance is an issue and you can't meet up any time soon consider chatting on the phone or getting a web cam.

- Don't jump into bed with someone straight away. Casual sex might seem like a good idea at the time but there is a downside in that it can make sex meaningless. Try to get to know each other as friends first and see if you are compatible and enjoy each other's company. You should always practise safe sex.

- Put some thought into topics of conversation and establish your boundaries early on. Are there issues that you don't particularly want to talk about? Stay within your limits until you know a person better.

- Develop your small talk. It puts everyone at ease and establishes common ground. Don't feel you have to impress by being smart or discussing worthy issues. Small talk is actually more intimate and it builds relationships more quickly.

• Keep yourself up to date with the latest news and entertainment. It will give you an opener to start talking to someone. Being informed and aware of what's going on in the world is also an attractive quality to have, as it shows you're not preoccupied with yourself.

• Pay attention to your body language and how other people see you. It is the biggest part of communication and what people judge you on in the first instance. If you're unsure how you come across ask a good friend for his or her opinion. You might be surprised. It's worth learning a few gestures or techniques to make you appear more open and confident. Try leaning forward slightly when you talk to someone and keeping up eye contact which will show that you are interested in what the other person is saying and will make you more approachable. Adopt them often enough and you will soon behave like that naturally.

- Take it slowly and make sure you're not on the rebound.

- Stay safe and always tell a friend where you are going and with whom, giving telephone numbers and addresses if you can. Try to meet people in the daytime initially and in public places rather than at either of your homes. Don't give out personal details about yourself too quickly.

- Show an interest in the person you are with. Listen to them and ask pertinent questions to show you've been listening. We all like talking about ourselves and by showing an interest in someone you become interesting to them.

- Always trust your instincts about people. These will be stronger if you're feeling grounded and relaxed. Meditation will be a great help here.

When to introduce a new partner to your children

It's entirely your call and whenever you feel ready. It depends on what kind of relationship you have with your children – how open it is and how much you tell them about your life. Have they accepted the split and moved on with their lives? If so, and they are happy that you are dating, then fine. Make it clear to them that you're meeting lots of new people and are just having fun and that you'll let them know if things get serious with someone. If, on the other hand, they are still hurting and angry about the break-up and you're not sure if the relationship is serious then leave it for a while. It's all about timing and you may feel they've had enough disruption for the moment. Trust your judgement on this one. You don't need to introduce your children to your new partner as a lover at first – you can say you're just friends. It's important not to overwhelm the children.

11

Practical lifelines

In this chapter we're going to look at a few of the practical things you'll need to consider if you're getting involved in a new relationship or think you might at some point in the future. Naturally you may be feeling a little anxious about your home and your finances – it is your security after all. If there are children to consider you may want to safeguard your assets for the futures of both yourself and the children. It's not exactly romantic to talk about the practicalities with a new partner but it is realistic and there are things you need to consider before getting married again or involved in another long-term relationship.

Your home

Here is a list of things you need to consider:

- Unlike spouses, a couple who live together do not have automatic rights to the family home – if you are planning on moving in with someone, or having someone move in to your house then the issue of home ownership should be discussed. If you and your new partner agree that you should both have an interest in the family home, you should see a solicitor, who can ensure that your wishes are properly reflected on the property deeds.

- Do you own or rent your current property? Is your new partner thinking about moving in with you to help you pay the mortgage? If so, it's best to have a cohabitation agreement in place stating clearly who pays the mortgage and who pays other bills. A new partner may try to claim a share in your property if he or she has paid towards the mortgage or made significant improvements to the house during their time living there. It doesn't matter if you each pay equal amounts for the mortgage, the bills and food. The person who pays the mortgage has all of the advantages.

- If you decide to move in with a new partner but don't intend to get married again then consider how much you have both paid towards the home. Cohabiting couples don't have the same legal rights and no matter how long you live together you won't be entitled to a fair share of the property unless you are joint tenants. If you don't want to or can't buy as joint tenants, meaning the proceeds would be split 50/50, then you can buy as 'tenants-in-common'. This means that you decide how much belongs to each other, for example, an 80/20 split. In this case, one of you pays 80 per cent of the house cost, the other 20 per cent. You'll therefore each get your fair share, if you part company, according to what you contributed in the first place. If you're buying together and are unsure what to do, talk to a solicitor.

Q: I was married for eight years and we split up some time ago. I've met someone else since then and it's quite serious but I can't get my head around the idea of us moving in together. She's quite messy for a start and I've got used to doing things my way around the house. I'm not sure I can go through all that again. Any suggestions?

A: Don't feel pressured into making a decision right now. What are both of your lifestyles like? When do you spend most of your time together? Some couples choose to 'live apart together' second time around – that is, they spend their weekends together and have their own lives and space during the week. This can work well if you're busy at work or both have previous relationships that still have some practicalities to sort out. If you own the property you might consider having a cohabitation agreement in place if your new partner does move in. This would spell out who pays the mortgage and who pays other utilities and will give you a little more peace of mind if you're worried about history repeating itself. It's natural to want to have your own space to live – especially as things ended badly with your wife and it has taken some time to sort out the house. Speak to your new partner and tell her your concerns.

Your finances

Once you get back on your feet, it's worth reviewing your financial position:

- How are your finances right now? Are things finalized with your ex-partner? Are there loose ends that need to be tied up? Even if the split was amicable it's worth making sure that you've agreed on what will happen to joint accounts, the house and any shared assets. If you were to inherit in the meantime, your ex-partner could potentially make a claim to part of that. Get things in writing and seek financial advice if you need to.

- If your ex-partner is currently paying you maintenance and you decide to remarry that may stop. Are you prepared for that financially? Have you spoken about it with your new partner and is he or she willing to help support you and your children, if you have them?

- Are there any further benefits you may be entitled to that you aren't currently claiming?

- Do you have a long-term financial plan? Do you have savings, a pension or investments and a will? How much would you like to have in the bank on your retirement?

• What sort of lifestyle do you want for yourself and your children if you have them? What about schooling? Where would you like to live? What steps can you take now to move towards your goals?

• Talk about money in the early stages and iron out any difficulties. If there is any debt how will you manage it? Do you want to be responsible for a partner's debts or have them registered at your address?

• Review your finances every three months and take independent advice if you're unsure about anything. Try to get into the habit of talking to each other about any issues so that problems don't build up.

Getting remarried

Falling in love again and remarrying is a wonderful thing, but there are practicalities to consider:

• Consider having a pre-nuptial agreement if you do have assets such as an inheritance or a business that you'd like to protect. It will clarify both of your rights in terms of these assets. Pre-nups aren't legally binding in the UK yet although at the time of writing steps are being made to address this and they do hold some influence in court. It is quite complicated, so seek legal advice. It involves both of you disclosing all of your assets and taking separate legal advice. It needs to be signed at least 21 days before the marriage takes place. The aim is to reach a fair and equal settlement for both of you.

- If you are still paying maintenance to your ex-partner and you go on to remarry you will still be required to make the payments. So, it's worth considering the financial implications of this if you have a new partner and stepchildren to support. Take some legal advice if you aren't sure.

- Review your pension and Will if you do remarry as they may be affected.

This is an overview of some of the practicalities you need to consider if you are involved in a new relationship or considering remarriage. Take some legal advice if you have specific concerns.

Q: I'm seeing someone new and feeling a little freaked out at the thought of having joint financial responsibility again. I had such a nightmare trying to get my ex-partner to pay bills on time and I'd like to have a bit of control over my money in the future. My partner thinks I've got trust issues and can't see what all the fuss is about. Am I being paranoid?

A: No. It's entirely normal to feel this way after a break-up if you had problems with money the first time around. Of course you want to set money aside for your future and you're probably feeling a lot more independent now and wary of what can go wrong. Talk to your partner about how you feel and the reasons why. Lots of couples keep their financial affairs separate and you could compromise by opening an extra joint bank account for household expenses and bills so that it feels like you're making some commitment together. You could also consider having a cohabitation agreement in place if you do decide to move in together which sets out who pays for what and who owns what in terms of property and assets.

The final two parts of the book are slightly different. Part 4 contains letters compiled from those of you who have written in to *This Morning*. Part 5 lists some useful organizations, websites, courses and books for further information so that you know where to go for specific help.

Part 4:
From the
Postbag

12

Your letters

No letters sent to *This Morning* are ever disclosed. The following letters are created from the hundreds we receive each week.

Dear Denise
My dad left my mum 12 months ago for a girl I used to be friends with. She is 25 and my dad is twice her age. My mum and dad had been together for 29 years and my mum is beside herself with pain. The last year has been the worst in our lives and each day seems to be getting harder. Mum cries all the time and desperately wants him back. She has recently started seeing a counsellor but it's not helping all that much. She says it can't bring dad back and that is all she wants. I am an only child and seeing her like this is killing me. I don't see my dad as I have so much hate for him for what he has done to us both. It isn't as though the girl is anything special and she doesn't have a nice nature. I can remember that from school. The thought of him with her is sickening and I'm having real difficulty coping.

Dear X

Thank you for your email. It must have been
an enormous shock for you and your mother
to learn that your father had been having an
affair. I can also appreciate that since she
was once your friend and is only your age it
may be more difficult for you to see her as
the woman she is as opposed to the girl you
knew. I'm afraid that your father may well
live to regret throwing away his marriage in
the years to come.

It will be difficult for a counsellor to make
headway while your mother can see only
one possible option but I hope you will
encourage your mum to keep going to
sessions in the hope of a breakthrough. It's
entirely understandable that after 25 years
she would find it difficult to contemplate
life without your father or come to terms
with what has happened but even if this
new relationship were to collapse there is no
knowing whether or not your father would
return. It has now been 12 months since
your father left so it's not a flash in the pan
and until your mother accepts this, the
healing process will not be able to start.

As long as she believes that his return is the only thing that can give the meaning back to her life then her unhappiness will persist and she will continue to be stuck in a state of limbo. I suspect that you spend a lot of time discussing what has happened and venting your understandable anger on both your dad and the other woman. As far as you can, try to avoid this. Don't refuse to discuss it but whenever possible talk about other things, perhaps a small change in the house or a holiday together.

Tell your mother that you have decided not to let them dominate your life and you hope she'll do the same because she is still a young woman. Encourage her to pamper herself and make sure she has nice perfume and gets her hair done occasionally. She needs to start seeing herself as a person again and not just the discarded half of a partnership. She also needs to discuss with her doctor whether or not she is depressed. If she is, and I suspect she may be, the doctor can really help.

Hopefully, in time, she will start accepting what has happened and stop pinning all hopes and future happiness on your father returning. Time will be the biggest healer for you both and it's important that you don't let your own life get sidelined. Ultimately, your happiness will be of great comfort to your mum. I wonder whether you are being supported by anyone while you are trying to support your mum? Careline (0845 122 8622) is a telephone counselling service for anyone who has a problem so do please think about giving them a call.

While I know that you may have felt powerless to help over the last year, just being there will have meant the world to her. If she wants to speak to someone else or wants to find other counselling should her present therapy come to an end, then Marriage Care (0845 660 6000) would be able to help. And take heart, this unhappy period will end eventually and you can both begin to live again.

Hi Denise

Please can you give me some advice on how to deal with my eight-year-old son? My husband of 15 years has decided he doesn't want to live with us anymore and my son has taken it really badly. At first he seemed to be coping well and then all of a sudden he has started to swear, pinch, punch, kick, threaten, draw on walls – the list goes on. The only person he does all these awful things to is my ten-year-old daughter, who has had her difficult moments dealing with her dad leaving but now has this to contend with too.

I can understand that this is a sign of 'anger' but I don't know how to deal with it. I have punished (which I didn't feel comfortable with), ignored and even just held him and told him how much I love him. This is totally out of character as he is normally such a good, loving child who is a pleasure to be around. His behaviour has thrown me totally. Also my daughter gets cross with me as I don't punish and she can't understand how he can get away with it. She also doesn't understand why he does all of this to her and gets very upset. I have been to see my doctor about it and he has referred us somewhere but there is such a long wait in between. I was hoping you might have some suggestions to steer

me in the right direction in the meantime.
Relations with their father are quite good and
they speak to him twice a day and see him three
times a week.

Dear X

I was very sorry to read that your marriage
has broken down. It sounds as if you have
been coping remarkably well but the
situation with the children won't be helping.
When a child's world changes suddenly it
throws them into confusion. Some become
silent and withdrawn, others try to turn the
clock back with 'bad' behaviour. Anger is
often fear in disguise and I wonder if your
son, having seen his father leave, is worried
that you might leave too? Clearly you
provide a loving home and he is in regular
contact with his father, but he is still an
eight-year-old child and can't be expected to
fully understand. It's possible that he might
blame himself or his sister for the break-up.
Children sometimes misguidedly believe
they are the cause of something going
wrong and so it is important that both you
and your husband make it clear that the
reasons you chose to live apart were solely

to do with the two of you and not them. Alternatively he may be angry at you for 'letting it happen' but fears showing this ('If I do then maybe Mummy will go too.').

The only other target to vent his feelings at is his sister, who he knows may not be able to put up much resistance. He might also hope that by being 'naughty' he will get your attention and any attention, good or bad, is attention. I am not suggesting in any way that you aren't giving them both lots of love and attention right now, but at this point when he feels so vulnerable and confused, however much you give may not feel like enough. Make it clear that physical attacks on his sister aren't acceptable but try not to punish. This is a confused little boy and not a bad one. Cuddle your daughter when you are alone together and ask for her patience but make sure she knows this won't go on forever.

I am pleased that you've taken the decision for him to have some counselling, but sorry to hear that this may take some time. In the interim it may be worth speaking to Young Minds (0800 018 2138) which offers support to any parent concerned about the emotional wellbeing of a child. They might also be able to offer alternative suggestions for support. Talking this through with Parentline Plus (0808 800 2222) might help too. His father should also be asked to help by explaining the situation and also giving as much attention to both children as he can. You both need to make sure that your daughter doesn't lose out when attention is given to your son. I'd also plan something, a short holiday or expedition, because having something to look forward to is a wonderful therapy. Give both children a share in decision making and responsibility and get your husband to support you in this. The focus needs to come off what has happened and on to good things which will happen in the future.

Dear Denise

Just over five years ago my husband of ten years was forced to reveal that he was having an affair with a colleague I believed was a platonic friend and he asked me for a divorce. Relate were very helpful during the time I had to stay in the home with my husband. He told me he was sorry that he had put me through all of this but when I suggested that he stop it and work on our marriage he said that things had gone too far and that he had made her promises.

I have now moved to another town and am happy with life (no relationship but I don't want one). My problem is that after five years I find that the pain and sadness have gone but I still feel terribly resentful – I want this feeling to go but it just doesn't. Because of my husband's behaviour I feel I cannot forgive – but do you think it would help if I did? My ambition is to reach a feeling of indifference. I thought this would have happened by now but it hasn't.

Dear X

Thank you for your letter. I think you're absolutely right to see indifference as the goal. Bitterness simply destroys peace of mind and only saints can forgive and feel affection for someone who has wronged them. But indifference only comes when the present life is so good that the old life is neither here nor there.

Over the years I have received many letters from people who have been hurt by someone close to them: hurt and angry, and anxiously wanting to know if, when and how they will ever be able to stop feeling that way. I think that part of their worry (and perhaps yours too) is that 'forgiving' the other person means they are somehow accepting what has happened and being weak. I don't think that forgiving means forgetting or letting the other person off the hook. It should mean that we are strong enough to take control of our lives and actively wish to move on. As long as you are thinking and worrying over what happened your ex-husband is still actively affecting your life and you continue to suffer. It is important that you let go of your feelings, so that you can start moving forward. After all, your ex-husband has taken a great deal from you already and it would be a real shame if he continued to deprive you of your peace of mind and happiness.

You say that counselling helped before and I would urge you to think about seeing someone again. If you want to have private counselling, contact the British Association for Counselling and Psychotherapy (0870 443 5252), which will put you in touch with those therapists in your area who specialize in relationship difficulties. In the meantime you can always call Marriage Care (0845 660 6000) which offers telephone support to anyone who is experiencing problems in their close personal relationships, whether married or not. Above all, start to make plans for the future and, while I appreciate you're not looking for another relationship, don't rule it out forever. Who knows what the future holds.

Dear Denise

I have been separated from my partner for four years. We have two lovely children aged five and eight but my ex-husband is still very bitter and twisted and I fear for the children and what effect his manipulation and lies will have on them. I divorced him for unreasonable behaviour as I no longer wanted to be his doormat and the children deserved better as he was very hostile towards them. He was so nice at first but everything changed the day we got married. Whatever I did or whatever I gave him was not enough. He is an only child and his mother was a big part of the problem. At first he saw the children regularly, coming round to bath them, but he didn't know how to as he had not done anything when we were together. I would always have to step in, as the children would end up crying. I asked him to start having contact with the children away from the home, for him to start getting to know them better. I thought this would make for a better relationship with him and his family and the children. He eventually agreed but still blamed me for everything and insisted I was getting rid of him. He always blames me for everything. I am always the bad guy!

I started seeing my present partner two years ago and fell very much in love. He has a child, a daughter, who lives with us. My ex went mad and told everyone that I had been seeing him while we were married, that I had had many affairs and done all sorts of bad things. This was to get everyone on his side. The anger got worse and he threatened my partner in front of the children, causing the police to be involved. Of course, that was all our fault too, he said we had started it and my partner had been the one doing the threatening. All lies. He has manipulated my friends with lies about me and my partner and has tried to break my family up too. He has taken the contact of our children to court four times because now there is nothing else that links us apart from them. He doesn't want to lose his hold over me.

When he has the children he lies and manipulates things and tells them he will take them to court when they are old enough to say who they want to live with. They are very confused when they return from him, but I try to make them happy, secure and comfortable at home. I now live with my partner and everything is going really well, they sleep well and their schoolwork is excellent. People tell me that if they were unhappy or confused etc. their schoolwork would suffer, but their father has nothing to do with their schooling, homework etc. I have done all of that on my own so far but fear that this might change if he gets his way.

I am having counselling myself and do suffer from anxiety and depression because of the fear of him winning (as everything is a competition to him and he needs to win). I would do anything for our children and constantly hope that one day he will move on and behave as agreed when first we separated. He has tried on many occasions to make my partner and I separate. I fear for what effect it will have on our children now and later on in life. Yes, he is their dad and I wish everything was amicable but he is having none of that. Please, please help me. We have tried mediation but he turned violent and it had to be discontinued.

Dear X

I was sorry to read about the problems you've been encountering since your separation. You suggest that the marriage itself was fraught with difficulties and so perhaps it was inevitable that when it broke down it would be a turbulent ride. I can appreciate how stressful the situation is and the worries you have for the children but it sounds as though you are more anxious than you need to be. I agree with the people you've spoken with that if the girls are doing well at school, sleep well and appear happy then they are. You have clearly built a secure and loving home with your partner and if they have this stability it will go a long way to offset any stress their father may be causing.

Your ex-partner may try to sabotage your happy home life, make threats, or tells lies, but if you carry on as normal, enjoying the time you spend with the girls, and going about your daily routines then the children will continue to feel safe and secure. As time goes on, it is likely that your ex-partner will tire of trying to disrupt your lives and will build a life of his own again. This will happen sooner if he sees he is wasting his time and does not upset you. He wants a reaction so try not to give him one but keep a note of everything that happens, as this could be useful if it ever came to court.

He will probably have a serious relationship at some time in the future and put his energies into that. Also, as the girls get older they will become less confused about his behaviour and less tolerant of it. The girls will have friends whose parents have split up too, and between them they will talk, make sense of what is happening and support one another.

I would urge you to continue with the counselling so that you have an outlet for your feelings. In the meantime, don't allow yourself to be turned inside out with worry by your ex. This is what he wants and the best form of retaliation is to get on with your lives, rise above it, and trust in all the signs that your children are happy. The less anxious you are for them, the more they will feel able to relax and cope with the situation.

Should you want some extra support then Parentline Plus (0808 800 2222) are always on hand. In the meantime, I wish you all the very best.

13

Your stories

My partner was very charismatic – well, he'd had four wives before me so that should have given me some idea! He was American and we met while I was travelling and living in South Africa. I came back to London and he moved over from the States to live with me. I think initially he enjoyed the thrill of the chase but as soon as he'd got me he stopped making the effort. Little cracks started to appear. For one thing, he was a workaholic and always away at the weekends.

I think in a relationship there is a defining moment when you realize that things aren't working out. For me it was when I was in hospital recovering from a breast operation and he came to visit. I was really ill and I remember him saying that he couldn't stay long as he hadn't enough money for the parking meter. It hit me then and I thought well, if you can't be with me now when I really need you then we don't have a future.

It was difficult but I left him shortly after and moved into a flat share with a girlfriend. Shortly afterwards she told me that she was pregnant and was planning to fly home to South Africa to have an abortion. For some reason this hit me really hard. I suppose I was grieving for the loss of her friendship and her baby as well as the loss of my relationship. It took me around six years to get over him properly and I kept things very light with men after that. There is a great book called 'The Power Of Positive Thinking' – it's full of affirmations and it helped me greatly.

Jamie

I've had four longish relationships, the longest being two years and nine months and the shortest, six months. I've learned something from each of them. What to expect, how a partner should and shouldn't treat you and how to discuss uncomfortable things.

My long-term relationship was failing and deep down I knew that. I also knew he was a little crazy and I was scared of breaking up with him. I was living with my parents at the time and they were key in making sure that I was okay. In the end he broke up with me and I didn't see it coming so took it very badly.

I don't think anything can prepare you emotionally for the raw emotion and upset that follow a break-up. There are a lot of tears but they subside after a while because it's so tiring to carry on crying! I then do lots of nice things

for myself – a facial, new pair of shoes, a
bunch of DVDs and a mammoth TV session
with hot chocolate and biccies. Never get a
haircut when you've just broken up – you'll
only regret it because you're not in a rational
frame of mind.

After a few days you realize that life goes on
and so must you. I carried on going to work as
that helped me to stop dwelling on it. I told the
girls in the office what had happened and that
I needed some time. They flocked around to
comfort me, usually with biscuits and tea! After
a couple of weeks the haze of emotion lifted
and I started to feel more normal. You become
more rational and start to do stuff again,
although little and often is better as you get
used to being on your own again because it
does feel weird not having your partner with
you. I recommend not drinking – when you're
drunk all you do is talk about the break-up and
think about it and you go all stupid again...

I always make lists. Me and my lists! Things
that I want to do now or that I couldn't do
when we were together because of him. It's a
good idea to do something radical like
skydiving or backpacking because you realize
that you can do things solo and it gives you

your confidence back. If that's not for you then find something that you used to enjoy doing as a child – a hobby or interest rather than sinking yourself into hours of shopping or eating or spending money you don't have. That won't give you the sense of comfort you need at this point.

Getting away is also a good idea – a place with new faces gives you distance on the whole 'couple' thing. You can be more objective about your own future, your plan of action and how to get closure. Hold off the drunken girly holidays until you're feeling more like your normal self and are fun to be around again.

I made sure he knew that I'd never see or speak to him again. Harsh I know but it was partly for my sanity and so I could have some power over the situation. He then contacted me a few weeks later wanting to give things another go. I didn't reply to his emails and hung up if he called. I deleted all of his details from my phone and email and put expensive gifts and photos in a shoebox to put up in the roof. The cheap gifts I sent back to him with no note. I try to be dignified but also brutal so that he knows how much it hurts.

Looking back it's a good thing that we split

up because I realize that ultimately I would never have had the life I wanted with him. Everything would have been on his terms and I would always be fighting for what I wanted to do. I would have been living his life not mine. I don't want to get to the end of my days and look back and see that I've compromised everything. I loved him very much but I didn't want to give things a second go. I had to love myself more and be kind to myself.

It takes courage to face up to things and I think that as you get older you become braver and less emotional about things. When you're young it's all about how you'll never love again. You realize that you chose a frog this time and that's okay because your prince is still out there looking for you.

Jane

14

Your thoughts and messages of hope

*Now that we're apart I keep
remembering how good it was in the
beginning and that hurts. I just have to
remind myself how bad it got in the end
and then I know I did the right thing.
But you do wonder when and if the pain
will stop.*

Sally

*I see him sometimes with his new
girlfriend and I wonder if she'll be like
me one day, deciding which photos to
keep and which to throw away. I won't
have so much room in the new house so
something has to go. But I'll be glad
when this place is sold and I move on.*

Emma

Getting divorced has given me back my identity and freedom. I feel strong now knowing that I can stand on my two feet, no matter what, and that I will survive. I'm not dependent on anyone for anything. Spend some time on your own getting to know yourself again and doing things that you enjoy.

Lisa

She told me quite coldly that she no longer loved me and would I please move out asap. She sounded like a stranger delivering an eviction notice. Everyone says I should put up a fight and say I'm staying but I can't live like this. I keep thinking about that Michael Jackson song '...how can eyes that shone so bright suddenly go so cold...' I think those are the words. Very apt.

Matt

The worst part was telling the kids but they were quite good about it really. Anyway, I was proud of them. They asked questions like where would they be and would they still see Dad. The fact that we'd talked it through beforehand and had the answers ready was a big help. I hope we can make it work for the kids' sake.

Jackie

At first we both said it would be amicable but gradually the nastiness crept in. I wish we'd done it legally earlier on. The plain fact is that divorce is messy and you can't get round that. Now that we're being practical and taking advice it's actually easier. But I'll still be heartily glad when it's over. There's a whole new world out there and for the first time in years I feel hopeful.

Si

Talking to the helpline made me realize that I wasn't the only person going through this and that helped. You feel like you're the only person in the world who's been dumped but in reality it happens to thousands of people.

Tofel

In hindsight I wouldn't have gone to mediation. I think it encourages men and women to be nice and kind and the woman goes along with it while the man carries on his own sweet way. I was encouraged to do mediation but I think I lost out financially as a result. It was all touch-feely and nice but ultimately, divorce is adversarial. I definitely feel that I lost out and wouldn't recommend it to other women. I think it leads to women getting a poorer deal – house- and maintenance-wise for the kids.

Liz

I am incredibly philosophical about it two years down the line. I have gone full circle and have had time to put the jigsaw pieces back together. I've since met someone who is my true love, my best friend and my partner in life.

Mike

Getting over it? I became a shopaholic. I should have got shares in Karen Millen instead! I had a great time on alcohol and sex. I started a new business and that took all my focus. I became more liberal and took away the 'good girl' image. The long-suffering wife became the independent woman in charge. Friends eventually told me to stop drinking and and I went to see a fantastic counsellor. I also went to Ecuador and did a life-changing trip in the Amazon.

Nazim

Many lessons:
Live with your partner for a long time
before getting married or having children.
Don't walk down the aisle before you
need to.
Don't gloss over their faults with
romantic notions.
Get to know everything about them.
Love – but watch who you give it to.

Frankie

It turns out his new partner is a
gynaecologist of all things. I'm afraid
that when I last spoke to him I couldn't
resist telling him that at least she could
show him where the clitoris and g-spot
are because he could never be bothered
to find that out for himself when we
were together!

Anne

It's good to get back on the bandwagon but not so fast that the new person 'doesn't compare' with the old. The best thing is to take down or destroy everything associated with your ex (pics, music, clothes) and to avoid going to all the places you used to hang out in together. Until you're ready, that is, to go back to those old haunts and superimpose your old experiences with bright, new happy ones. I think the key thing to realize is that when you are younger you can easily drift in and out of relationships that are comfortable but not really about love and there is a huge difference between the two. As you get older you realize that love doesn't conquer all and that there is much more to a relationship or marriage than love or sex – and that you need to have a partner who recognizes that. If they don't then you need to be brutally honest and ask yourself if this person is the person who will always be there for you. If you doubt that then you need to find someone who will. You deserve that and so do they.

Kelly

Part 5: More Help at Hand

This section contains some useful contacts, websites and books for practical and emotional support.

15

Useful contacts

General

Aquila
Tel: 01892 665 524
www.aquilatrust.org
Network of divorce support groups.

British Association for Counselling and Psychotherapy
BACP House
15 St John's Business Park
Lutterworth
Leicestershire LE17 4HB
Tel: 0870 443 5252
Therapy for adults and children.

British Association for Sex and Relationship Therapy (BASRT)
Tel: 0208 543 2707
email: **info@basrt.org.uk**
Provides an information service, and will help you to find a therapist in your area.

CALM (Campaign Against Living Miserably)
Tel: 0800 585 858
www.thecalmzone.net
Helpline for men aged between 15 and 35.

Care for the Family

Tel: 02920 810 800

www.careforthefamily.org.uk

A nationwide support helping you and your family through good and bad times.

Careline

Cardinal Heenan Centre

326 High Road, Ilford

Essex IG1 1QP

Tel: 0845 122 8622 (Monday to Friday 10 a.m. to 1 p.m. and 7 p.m. to 10 p.m.)

Provides a telephone counselling service for individuals in distress and suffering from relationship difficulties, depression, mental health or domestic violence.

Citizens Advice Bureau (CAB)

www.citizensadvice.org.uk

www.adviceguide.org.uk

One-stop centre for advice on your rights regarding property, divorce, cohabitation, legal rights, finance and children.

Community Service Volunteers (CSV)

237 Pentonville Road

London N1 9NJ

Tel: 0207 278 6601
www.csv.org.uk
Information on different types of voluntary work.

Depression Alliance
212 Spitfire Studios
63–71 Collier Street
London N1 9BE
Tel: 0845 123 2320
www.depressionalliance.org
Provides information packs on depression.

Divorce Care
www.divorcecare.com
Seminars and support groups to help adults and children understand divorce and its effects.

Divorce Recovery Workshops
07000 781 889
www.drw.org.uk
Nationwide courses consisting of six weekly evenings to help you come to terms with divorce.

Family Contact Line
Mayors Road, Altrincham
Cheshire WA15 9RP

Tel: 0800 085 3330

www.napac.org.uk

Telephone listening support and counselling for those dealing with relationship difficulties and marital problems.

Families Need Fathers

www.fnf.org.uk

Support for divorced and separated parents on shared parenting issues.

Gingerbread

Tel: 0800 018 4318

www.gingerbread.org.uk

Free advice and information for lone parents.

Home Start

2 Salisbury Road

Leicester LE1 7QR

Tel: 0116 233 9955

www.home-start.org.uk

Provides support for families across the UK.

Infertility Network UK

Charter House

43 St Leonards Road

Bexhill-on-Sea

East Sussex TN40 1JA
Tel: 08701 188 088
www.infertilitynetworkuk.com
Provides advice, support and information for
people who are dealing with infertility.

International Coach Federation
UK ICF
248 Walsall Road
Bridgtown
Cannock
Staffs WS11 0JL
Tel: 0870 751 8823
www.coachfederation.org.uk

Marriage Care
1 Blythe Mews
Blythe Road
London W14 0NW
Tel: 0845 660 6000
www.marriagecare.org.uk
Help and support counselling for those with
relationship difficulties.

National Association for Voluntary and Community Action

The Tower
2 Furnival Square
Sheffield S1 4QL
Tel: 0114 278 6636
www.navca.org.uk
Promotes local voluntary and community action nationally.

National Council for the Divorced and Separated

51 Jubilee Way, Necton
Swaftham PE37 8LZ
Tel: 0704 147 8120
www.ncds.org.uk
Information, support and social events for the divorced and separated. Contact the National Secretary for events in your area.

National Council for One-Parent Families

255 Kentish Town Road
London NW5 2LX
Tel: 0800 018 5026
A helpline promoting the welfare of lone parents and their children.

National Debtline
Tricorn House
51–53 Hagley Road
Birmingham B16 8TP
www.nationaldebtline.co.uk
Provides free confidential and independent
advice on how to deal with debt problems.

National Family Mediation
7 The Close, Exeter
Devon EX1 1EZ
Tel: 01392 271 610
www.nfm.org.uk
Network of mediation services for all members of
the family and extended family

National Federation of Plus Areas of Great Britain
201 Commerce House, High Street
Sutton Coldfield B72 1AB
Tel: 0870 874 7587
www.18plus.org.uk
Social activities for those aged 18–35.

NHS Direct
Tel: 0845 4647
www.netdoctor.org.uk
Provides general help on medical matters.

National Institute of Medical Herbalists (NIMH)
Elm House
54 Mary Arches Street
Exeter EX4 3BA
www.nimh.org.uk
Tel: 01392 426 022

One Up
PO Box 9449
Earls Colne
Colchester C06 2WT
Tel: 01787 223 557
www.oneupmagazine.co.uk
Magazine for single parents and step-parents.

Parentline Plus
520 Highgate Studios
53–79 Highgate Road
Kentish Town
London NW5 1TL
Tel: 0808 800 2222
www.parentlineplus.org.uk
Helpline for anyone in a parenting role including step- and lone parents.

Relate

Herbert Gray College
Little Church Street
Rugby CV21 3AP
Tel: (Bookings) 01788 573 241
www.relate.org.uk
Relationship counselling for individuals and couples. Runs a course called 'Moving Forward: after a divorce or break-up'.

REACH

89 Albert Embankment
London SE1 7TP
Tel: 0207 582 6543
Part-time voluntary opportunities for professionals.

The Samaritans

Tel: 08457 90 90 90 (local rate)
www.samaritans.org.uk
email: **jo@samaritans.org**
Confidential listening support for anyone in crisis.

Shelter
88 Old Street
London EC1V 9HU
Tel: 0808 800 4444
www.shelter.org.uk
Housing law and your rights, and relationship breakdown.

Tavistock Centre for Couple Relationships
Tel: 0208 938 2372
www.tccr.org.uk
Working towards improving the quality of adult relationships and preventing family breakdown. Offers relationship counselling, couples psychotherapy, sex therapy, divorce and separation therapy, training and short courses, and research.

The Institute of Family Therapy
24–32 Stephenson Way
London NW1 2HX
Tel: 0207 391 9150
www.instituteoffamilytherapy.org.uk
Provides clinic and family mediation services.

Volunteering England

Regent's Wharf

8 All Saints Street

London N1 9RL

Tel: 0845 305 6979

www.volunteering.org.uk

Information on different types of voluntary work.

2-in-2-1 Limited

11 Lamborne Close

Sandhurst

Berks GU47 8JL

www.2-in-2-1.co.uk

Advice and articles on shaping, enriching, maintaining and repairing your relationship.

Young Minds

48–50 St John Street

London EC1M 4DG

Tel: 0800 018 2138 (Parent information line)

www.youngminds.org.uk

Helpline for adults with concerns about the mental health of a child or young person.

Domestic Violence

Mankind

Tel: 0870 794 4124

www.mankind.org.uk

Support for men suffering domestic abuse.

Men's Advice Line

Tel: 0808 801 0327

www.mensadviceline.org.uk

Help and advice for men experiencing domestic abuse.

Refuge

Tel: 0808 2000 247 (24-hour helpline)

www.refuge.org.uk

Advice, support and refuge housing for women experiencing domestic violence.

Women's Aid

Tel: 0808 2000 247 (free 24-hour helpline)

www.womensaid.org.uk

National charity working to end domestic violence against women and children.

Legal

The Divorce Bureau
Tel: 0800 731 9831
A free service that matches you with a local solicitor if divorcing.

Law Centres Federation
Duchess House
18–19 Warren Street
London W1T 5LR
Tel: 0207 387 8570
www.lawcentres.org.uk
Will provide contact details for law centres near you.

Rights of Women
Tel: 0207 251 6577 (legal advice line)
www.rightsofwomen.org.uk
Provides advice on all aspects of relationship breakdown and divorce, including help with children and contact issues, domestic and sexual violence. Offers free legal advice sheets and a 'find a solicitor' service.

16

Helpful websites

Children

www.itsnotyourfault.org (for children who are going through a break-up)
www.thesite.org (information and support for young people aged 16–25)

Dating

www.dating-agencies-uk.co.uk (provides an overview of introduction agencies)
www.single-living.com
www.parship.co.uk
www.parentsalready.com (for single parents)
www.kno.org.uk – Kids No Object (for single parents)
www.datingforparents.com
www.match.com
www.friendsreuniteddating.com
www.udate.com
www.speeddater.co.uk
www.drawingdownthemoon.co.uk
www.onlylunch.co.uk
www.loveandfriends.com
www.mysinglefriend.com

Divorce and break-up

www.advicenow.org.uk/livingtogether
(checklist for those going through a break-up)
www.oneplusone.org.uk
www.divorcemag.com
www.divorceaid.co.uk
www.armchairadvice.co.uk (advice on
relationships)
www.itsallabouteggontoast.co.uk (for men
going through a break-up)
www.divorceandchildren.com
www.equalparenting.org
www.wifesgone.com
www.therelationshipgym.com
www.grandparentsapart.co.uk
www.webpysch.com (psychologist Nancy
Wesson's lifecycle of a relationship)
www.bbc.co.uk/relationships
www.channel4.com/health (useful advice on sex
and relationships)
www.soyouvebeendumped.com

Domestic violence

www.emotionalabuserecoverynow.com
(provides help for those suffering domestic
violence)
www.cri.org.uk (Crime Reduction Initiatives:
Open the Door on Domestic Abuse)

Finance

www.moneyfacts.co.uk
www.unbiased.co.uk (independent financial
advice)
www.cccs.co.uk (Consumer Credit Counselling
Service – offers help for those in financial
distress)
www.directgov.uk (comprehensive public
service information)
www.pensionsadvisoryservice.org.uk (non-
profit-making organizaton providing free
information and advice)

Health

www.netdoctor.org.uk
NHS Direct – 0845 4647 (provides general help
on medical matters)

Legal

www.adviceguide.org.uk (your rights – Citizens Advice Bureau)
www.clsdirect.org.uk (Community Legal Service Direct – advice and help with legal aid)
www.hmcourts-service.gov.uk (legal information regarding divorce)
www.sfla.co.uk (simple free law adviser)

Parenting

www.loneparents.org
www.mumsnet.com
www.stepfamilies.co.uk

Personal and professional development

www.women-returners.co.uk (provides advice, contacts and help for women returning to the workplace after a career break)
www.onelifelive.co.uk (offers exhibitors, workshops and seminars to give you practical advice on creating a new life for yourself)
www.coachfederation.org (International Coach Federation – worldwide resource for business and personal life coaches)

www.themarriagecourse.org (provides learning
tools for a healthy marriage)
www.bni.com (Business Networking
International – the largest business networking
organization in the world)
www.chamberofcommerce.com (Chamber of
Commerce – offers full resource guide, and a
section for children and parents as well as advice
on how to do better business)
www.vso.org.uk (voluntary work overseas)
www.navca.org.uk (the National Association for
Voluntary and Community Action, promoting
local voluntary and community action nationally)
www.learndirect.co.uk (online courses for
professional development)
www.readinggroups.peoplesnetwork.gov.uk
(offers advice on how to find or start a local
reading group)
www.open.ac.uk (Open University for distance
learning)

Pet charities

www.animalrescuers.co.uk
www.pdsa.org.uk
www.rspca.org.uk
All help with pet are and finding new homes.

Travel/holidays

www.thelmaandlouise.com (day trips and holidays for female travellers)
www.single-living.com
www.friendshiptravel.com
www.solosholidays.co.uk
www.explore.co.uk
www.smallfamilies.co.uk
www.solitairhols.co.uk/
www.travelone.co.uk/
www.mangoholidays.co.uk
www.pgl.co.uk
www.adventurecompany.co.uk
www.ramblers.org.uk

Useful books

After the Affair – Julia Cole, 2001 (Relate Guides)

Find Your Way Through Divorce – Jill Curtis, 2001 (Help Yourself)

Gap Years for Grown Ups – Susan Griffith, 2006 (Vacation Work)

Helping Children Cope With Divorce (Overcoming Common Problems) – Rosemary Wells, 2003 (Sheldon Press)

How to Mend a Broken Heart – Christine Webber, 2004 (Help Yourself)

Moving On: Breaking Up Without Breaking Down – Suzie Hayman, 2001 (Relate Guides)

Networking: The Art of Making More Friends – Carole Stone, 2001 (Vermillion)

Starting Again: How to Learn from the Past for a Better Future – Sarah Litvinoff, 2001 (Relate Guides)

The Power of Positive Thinking – Norman Vincent Peale, 1990 (Vermillion)

The 'Which?' Guide to Divorce: Essential Practical Information for Separating Couples – Imogen Clout, 2005 (Which Consumer Guides)

When Your Relationship Ends (Rebuilding Books for Divorce and Beyond) – Bruce Fisher, 2005 (Impact Publishing)

Your Money or Your Life: A Practical Guide to Solving Your Financial Problems and Affording a Life You'll Love – Alvin D. Hall, 2003 (Coronet Books)

CONCLUSION

We hope this book has been useful in helping you to move forward and come to terms with your past relationships. Hopefully you feel that you know yourself a lot better emotionally and are aware of the financial and practical aspects of living with another person. Relationships are very important but they are only one aspect of your life and they don't make you a balanced individual. You need to do that yourself through your interests, friendships, travel and work. Whether you feel ready to date again or not, concentrate your efforts on rebuilding those other areas and your networks to create a life that *you* really want and feel happy with rather than fitting into someone else's plans. It can be very easy to lose sight of yourself when you're in a long-term relationship.

Be kind to yourself and appreciate the small things that each day brings. Having peace of mind, solitude and time to reflect on your life and set new goals is essential for your health and wellbeing. It is very empowering to know that happiness is something you have achieved for yourself through your friends, interests and pursuits and that you are not reliant on a partner to make you happy. Your life is a wonderful adventure and there will be many good times ahead as well as wonderful people to share in your journey. Dip into this book whenever you feel you need a bit of reassurance on a low day. Everyone associated with it wishes you well in your new life.

Also available from *This Morning* and Hodder Education are:

- This Morning: Escape Domestic Violence

- This Morning: Get Out of Debt

- This Morning: Beat Your Depression

- This Morning: Cope With Bereavement

- This Morning: Cope With Infertility

- This Morning: Overcome Your Postnatal Depression

- This Morning: Beat Your Addiction